Let God Chart Your Course!

BY

DR. WILLIAM F.R. GILROY, D.MIN

Table of Contents

Dedication

*For Nancy and
Bill, Brad, Alexis, Missy, Aiden, Hailey, Hunter, and Blake
With gratitude, love and thanksgiving for all that you have
meant and continue to mean to me!*

Acknowledgement

I owe a great deal of thanks to my sister Betty for all she has done to support and encourage me as I wrote this memoir. Her work as my editor has been exceptional. I benefited immensely from her expertise and treasure the opportunity this effort has given us to work together in such a special way. I know our parents, Bill and Doris Gilroy, would be proud!

Introduction

"God blessed them, and God said to them, 'Be fruitful and multiply, and fill the earth and subdue it; and have dominion over the fish of the sea and over the birds of the air and over every living thing that moves upon the earth.'"

GENESIS 1:28

"Now the Lord said to Abram, 'Go from your country and your kindred and your father's house to the land that I will show you. I will make of you a great nation, and I will bless you and make your name great, so that you will be a blessing.'"

GENESIS 12:1-2

"…God called to him out of the bush, 'Moses, Moses!' And he said, 'Here I am.' …Then the Lord said, 'I have observed the misery of my people who are in Egypt;…. Indeed, I know their sufferings, and I have come down to deliver them from the Egyptians, and to bring them up out of that land to a good and broad land, a land flowing with milk and honey…. So come, I will send you to Pharoah to bring my people, the Israelites, out of Egypt.'"

EXODUS 3:4-10

"Now the word of the Lord came to Jonah…, saying, 'Go at once to Nineveh, that great city, and cry out against it; for their wickedness has come before me.'"

JONAH 1:1-2

"As he walked by the Sea of Galilee, he saw two brothers, Simon, who is called Peter, and Andrew his brother, casting a net into the sea – for they were fishermen. And he said to them, 'Follow me, and I will make you fish for people.'"

ST. MATTHEW 4:18-19

"And Jesus came and said to them, 'All authority in heaven and on earth has been given to me. Go therefore and make disciples of all nations, baptizing them in the name of the Father and of the Son and of the Holy Spirit, and teaching them to obey everything that I have commanded you. And remember, I am with you always, to the end of the age.'"

ST. MATTHEW 28:18-20

Throughout Biblical history God has openly communicated with his people. He speaks to Adam and Eve and gives them directions for the living of their lives. He instructs Abraham to leave his home and family and travel to a new and mysterious land, where he will become the "father" of a great nation and a person who will eventually be both revered and honored. He calls to Moses from a burning bush and sends him on a mission to free the Israelites from their Egyptian captivity. He tells Jonah to go to Nineveh and speak out against the sinful ways of the people living there and foretell of their doom. And Jonah is just one of many, known as the prophets, to whom God spoke and gave direction, and who, in turn, spent a good portion of their lives sharing God's Word with God's people.

God's Word then takes on human flesh in His only Son, Jesus Christ, and in a most close up and personal way, God not only speaks to His people but also shares completely in their lives. In and through Jesus the guidance and direction continues. Disciples are called and instructed and sent out to minister to others and to proclaim God's "good news" as it is now made manifest in Jesus. And when the mission of Jesus is finished here on earth, and He prepares to return to His Father in heaven, a great commandment or commission is issued for all believers in Christ to hear to make disciples of all peoples and to teach them to obey all that God has commanded.

God in Jesus then makes a promise, "I will always be with you," Jesus says, "even to the end of time."

Obviously, God has always wanted to be in touch with the children He so dearly loves. He desires to be a part of our lives, to provide guidance, to give direction, to inspire our actions, and to show us how we can best use the talents with which He has blessed us for the good of others. That is certainly clear in the scriptures, as time and time again, we read stories confirming how God interacts with man.

Today, however, we may well wonder if God still desires to speak to us. Perhaps we look at the world today and wonder how a loving God would ever wish to interact with such an unloving group of people. The evil ways of the world are certainly contrary to God's will for us, and so we might not even blame God for not speaking to us any longer. There are, after all, times when we, too, refrain from speaking to or interacting with those who have hurt us in one way or another, and surely our actions must bring God an inordinate amount of pain.

But, as Jesus promised and as He has shown with great consistency, God does not forsake us or abandon us. Instead, He remains with us constantly and will do so to the end of time. Because God loves us in spite of ourselves, He will never leave us alone to flounder in our own cesspool of sin and despair but will constantly seek to reaffirm His love for us, and to show us what it is He desires for us in life.

Being the people we are, however, we tend to look for tangible, visible evidence. We want our own "burning bush" experience; we want our own "face-to-face" with God; we want to be told directly not "to eat the fruit of that tree" or to go to today's equivalent of Nineveh (and there are so many from which we might choose) to be a spokesperson for God. Absent such experiences we might, indeed, continue to question over time God's ability or even willingness to communicate so openly with us today, as He once did with those whose stories are recounted for us in the scriptures. And absent such experiences, we might also begin to question the reality of God's continuing presence with us.

Throughout the following chapters, I will endeavor to take you on a journey, the goal of which is to open your ears, your eyes, and your hearts to the truth of God's continuing, constant, and consistent presence in our lives. Through reflection of my life and ministry, I hope to enable you to develop an enlightened understanding of how God does involve Himself in our lives on a daily basis, communicate with us so that we might better understand His will for us, and guide us, if we will allow Him to do so, down the pathways that are best for us to follow and which will lead us to experience the fullest, most meaningful, and blessed life possible.

As I have discovered, God is extremely active in our lives. He speaks to us and makes His will known to us daily through those around us and through unique and often wonderfully mysterious experiences. He reveals Himself to us in so many ways, so that His constant presence with us, even in the darkest of times, might be felt.

Hopefully, you will recognize, as you follow my story, the many ways God has spoken and continues to speak to you as well, and as a result you will realize anew how God is with you. He always will be, if you are open to His guidance in your life.

My Glory All The Cross

I have often wondered about that one special moment that changed my life! Was it kismet? Was it God's will being manifested? Or are kismet and God's will sometimes uniquely synonymous? Whatever it was, however, it has remained a defining moment for me – one I have often shared with others and one that will forever remind me of how God does indeed reach out to us in often mysterious ways to guide and direct our lives. There is just no other way to explain the "call" I one day received!

It was the early 1960's; I was in my early to mid-teens and consequently incapable of fully understanding the implications of what had occurred. It all happened within the context of a retreat I was attending with the youth from my church. I was raised a Lutheran, and the youth ministry program at that time was referred to as the Luther League. It was our practice to spend a weekend every fall

1

and every spring at a camp called Mar-Lu-Ridge, which was located on a mountain just outside of Frederick, Maryland.

In all honesty, the programs normally developed for those weekends never inspired my attendance or participation. The reason I went was just to have some fun with my peers and to enjoy some female companionship unavailable to me throughout the week, since I attended the Boys' Latin School of Maryland, a private boys' school in Baltimore. A day arrived on one of those retreats when there was some free time in the schedule. I wanted some quiet time away from the company of my friends, so I took a hike on a trail that afforded me a spectacularly beautiful view of the Potomac River as it flowed out of Harper's Ferry, West Virginia, and made its way south through the adjoining states of Maryland and Virginia. It is a view that, to this day, inspires me, and now, as then, remains a view I seek to enjoy whenever I happen to be at Mar-Lu-Ridge.

Walking alone through the woods that day, I found a spot where I was truly separated from the noise and activities of all the others and took a moment to lean against a tree just to enjoy, for a time, that majestic vista as it spread out before me in the valley below. Mesmerized by what I was seeing, I became lost in the wonder of God's creation.

After a few minutes of enjoying the view, something in my peripheral vision distracted me. Right above my shoulder in the bark of the tree was a tiny, jeweled cross. It obviously had little material value. It was something which, in those days, could easily be purchased at what was known as a five and dime store, a place for less expensive items. And the fact that someone had left it wedged into the bark of a tree confirmed my conclusion that what I held in my hand was certainly no treasure – at least in a material sense.

But it did stir up some questions. How long had it been there? Who had placed it there? And why out of all the trees in that mountaintop forest had I decided to lean against the one that held the cross?

Naturally I had no answers to those rhetorical questions, so I just examined the little cross I held. As I did, I noticed a hole in the center of the cross. Peering through that hole, I discovered that inside the cross was a printed version of the Lord's Prayer. Barely an inch and three-quarters in height, that little cross remarkably held some very special words for all to see if they would but look.

I also made a decision. Right or wrong, I concluded that the cross now belonged to me and placed it in my pocket. Perhaps I should have left it where I found it for someone else to discover and ponder for a while, but that was not my decision. My decision was to keep it.

Eventually, however, the novelty of the cross in my pocket wore off. I'm sure I shared my story with my parents and my sister, and maybe others as well, but soon the cross was relegated to a jewelry box in my room where it remained among my cuff links, old watches, and perhaps a toy soldier or two while I went through my high school years and on to college.

Why it was never discarded or lost I don't know. While I was away at school, my parents sold the house where I had grown up and moved out of Baltimore to a new home in a community near Annapolis, Maryland. As my parents prepared for their move, many old items from my youth were discarded. The cross, however, survived that purge and remained in my possession. And even though it wasn't always physically within my reach, it was with me spiritually, and in that sense, it possessed me more than I possessed it.

My original intention for attending college and seeking a degree was to become a teacher and coach. It was my hope that one day I would be able to return to Boys' Latin, the preparatory school from which I had graduated, and become a member of its faculty. As a result, I decided to major in physical education and began my career path at Lenoir Rhyne College in Hickory, North Carolina.

It wasn't long, however, before I realized that I was making a mistake. Though Lenoir Rhyne was small, it had a very successful football team and a more than adequate basketball team. Most of the athletes were physical education majors, and most of the professors in that area were coaches whose jobs depended, for the most part, on the success of the teams they coached. Though I longed to eventually be a coach as well, the courses I was taking were not all that challenging for me, and I began to believe that I would be wasting my father's tuition money should I continue on that path and, at the same time, denying myself a more complete education.

I, therefore, changed both my major as well as my career aspirations. I chose history as the course of study I would pursue and decided I wanted to be a lawyer. I also chose to major in German. It had been the language I had taken in prep school, and since I tested so well on my freshman year placement exams, I was enrolled in an advanced German course, as I embarked on the journey to fulfill my two year language requirement. Recognizing my situation, the German professor offered me the opportunity to be his student assistant and encouraged me to major in German as well. Because of my advanced placement, it would be a major I could complete by the end of my junior year. I took him up on the offer and pursued a double major from that moment on, with every intention to enter law school once my undergraduate years were over.

In the midst of my junior year, however, those plans changed again. Though I felt content with my career goals and was extremely happy with my college experience, I began to realize a time in my life that was both puzzling and distressing. And the source of it all was that cross. In a very real sense it began to haunt me.

As I lay in bed at night, I began to think about my future. The United States was in the midst of a war in Vietnam, and there was still a nationwide draft of young men eligible for military service. As a student, I was deferred from that draft, but upon graduation I would become eligible. Several of my fraternity brothers had begun to look into Officer Candidate School opportunities, as did I. For a time, I considered the Marine Corps program and discussed it with my parents prior to the beginning of my third year of college.

I honestly had no real feelings or thoughts about whether the war in Vietnam was a "just" war, but I did know it was extremely controversial, and something that had divided the country. Some of my fellow students had already been in combat there and had even been wounded, but in the South in the late 1960's there didn't seem to be the anti-war protests that were so prevalent in the North. Southerners are extremely conservative, I think, and so our campus was spared some of the ordeals experienced by other campuses across the country, as students battled with authorities in militant protests against what many considered an unjust and unnecessary war.

I was also the product of a conservative family that believed in this country. Both my father and my uncle had served in the United States Army during World War II, and both had answered the call to service without hesitation.

As a result, I was willing to serve as well, if my country needed me, and that's why I had joined my friends who were considering the Officer Candidate Programs that would be available to us when we had attained our degrees.

With all those thoughts on my mind, my nights became more than a bit restless. I then started to have a recurring dream. In that dream I found myself leaning against that tree on the mountaintop and discovering that little cross. Night after night that dream returned, and I began to wonder why. It had been several years since I had found the cross. I wasn't the same person I had been when the cross first appeared in my life, and in many ways, I had put that experience behind me. Or, at least, that's what I believed.

Suddenly, however, it was back in my life, and I struggled to determine why. Was it all just a trick of my subconscious – a remembrance of a "certain" time now long gone as I anticipated an uncertain future? Or, was it something more? Was it possible that God was speaking to me in that dream and that I needed to listen to what was being said? Was God in some way "calling" me?

I had never really considered the ministry as a career – at least not seriously – even though the visitation pastor of my home church would often encourage me to pursue it. Serving as an acolyte, or altar boy, on Sunday mornings, he would ask, from time to time, if I was taking Latin in school. And when I would tell him I was, he would say, "That's good because it may be of help to you when you go to seminary." Still, I had no plans to go. Though I enjoyed being active at the church, I really didn't like public speaking and could never envision myself having to preach a sermon every week. But apparently he had planted a seed, and as I remembered his words and strove to interpret my dreams, I grew ever more troubled and confused.

One weekend I drove home from Hickory, North Carolina, to Annapolis, Maryland. I took a Friday off and left Thursday after my classes were over and drove the nearly five hundred miles in order to keep an appointment I had made with the pastor of my church. His son was my brother-in-law, who, was at that time in his second year of seminary, so he was more than my pastor; he was also, to some extent, a part of my family.

Meeting with him on Friday morning in the church parlor, I explained the personal turmoil I had been experiencing. I spoke of the cross and of the dreams and of the difficulty I was having as I attempted to interpret what it all meant for me. Being the good pastor he was, he listened quietly and reflectively, and when I was finished he asked, "Don't you think God might be calling you to enter the ministry?" And although I was almost frightened to say the word, I answered, "Yes!"

It was a big decision for me. I had never ever envisioned going to seminary and becoming a pastor. I wasn't sure I could do it. I wasn't even totally sure I wanted to. But it just seemed right to me for some reason, and I left church that day feeling anxious but good.

With my pastor's help I started the process which would lead to my being accepted to seminary upon graduation from college. The dreams stopped, and I felt more and more at peace with my decision as I moved on toward that goal.

I visited with my sister and brother-in-law in Gettysburg, Pennsylvania, where he was a seminary student and learned more about what my future would hold in terms of my academic requirements and practical experiences.

I thought about what the ministry might be like for me and what I really wanted to do. And since I had considered post-college military service, I decided that the young men and women of our nation's armed services were the ones to whom I wanted to minister, so I began to think of a career as a military chaplain.

My last few semesters of college flew by, and I began to look forward to a new challenge and to life as a seminarian. Never could I have ever imagined how significant a role the little cross I found embedded in the bark of a tree on a mountaintop would play in setting the course my life would eventually take. But I did learn from the experience that God does indeed speak to us in often strange and wonderful ways, and we do our best in life when we take the time to listen.

I also learned that with God, anything is possible. Even a shy, less than confident, introvert can be inspired and called to serve Him in so many wonderful ways. As you read on, I hope you will see that truth for yourself, and perhaps realize as well that God has been speaking to you, too.

Right Place - Right Time

The Lutheran Theological Seminary in the little town of Gettysburg, Pennsylvania approximately ninety minutes from Baltimore, Maryland, and Washington, D.C., is the oldest Lutheran Theological Seminary in the country and the only one in a rural setting. Seminary Ridge, for those familiar with the Civil War era, was the site where the famous Battle of Gettysburg began, and to this day, the three buildings that were there during the battle remain a part of the campus. Considering the anti-war and anti-military climate of the late 1960's and early 1970's, I found the location of the Seminary to be ironic, and yet it is because of the history of Gettysburg that I chose to matriculate at precisely that institution.

Seminary, however, was a challenge for me! Academically I held my own, but socially it was something of a shock. I had visited the Lutheran Seminary in Columbia, South Carolina, while in college and knew that several of my fraternity brothers, who also felt called to the ministry, were studying there. Joining them would have been easy for me and would have offered me, in a social way, the opportunity to continue with the college experience I had so enjoyed. But, I opted to return north in order to be closer to family, and to be able to study in a place that so interested me as a lover of history.

In college I had been a member of what was undoubtedly, at that time, the best fraternity on campus. And though I'm sure there are others that would claim that distinction, my fraternity's record speaks for itself. It annually won the awards given to the Greek organizations for academic achievement. It excelled in inter-Greek athletic events, as well as choral competitions, and its members held many of the class and campus-wide elected offices. In so many ways, the members of my fraternity were campus leaders and a fun-loving group. The camaraderie was special and to this day, many of us remain very close.

Seminary was a totally different kind of experience. Many of my peers were married and consequently, not only had their studies to focus on, but also, in order to support their families, had part-time jobs. This reality tended to divide the student body, especially in one of the dorms where the married students lived directly below the single students. And since the single students were more "care-free" and tended to party and joke around a bit, the noise on that floor frequently disturbed the families on the floor below, which, in turn, created tension between the two disparate groups.

In addition, the war in Vietnam was the source of a great deal of national discontent, especially on college campuses in the North. The Seminary was no exception. The protests there were not violent, by any means, but there were students ready to march against the war and who were quite outspoken in their beliefs. It was during my first year in Seminary that the Kent State event occurred. The gunning down of protesting students on the Kent State campus by members of the Ohio National Guard was a tragedy that inspired members of the Seminary student body to plan a march to the peace light, which burned perpetually on the Gettysburg Battlefield, with the intention of extinguishing that flame.

The decision to attend seminary in Gettysburg left me to flounder a bit, as I struggled to adapt to a campus experience and life totally different from that with which I was more familiar. I was also something of an anomaly on that campus. My intention, after all, was to pursue ordination into the ministry of Word and Sacrament and eventually become a chaplain in the U.S. Navy, which, as one might imagine, did not sit well with my peers. It was a time of struggle for me both emotionally and spiritually. It was a struggle to find a common ground on which to stand with my fellow students without compromising my own principles and beliefs. And fortunately I found that ground, and in that discovery, I also found acceptance and new friends.

As it turned out, the sports program at the seminary provided me not only with the opportunity to release the tension I was experiencing, but also to open the door to some new relationships, which proved to be so important to me.

Sports have always been an outlet for me. In high school I competed in football, basketball, lacrosse and tennis. I played on fraternity teams in college and was invited to try out for the college basketball team, and had overtures from some of the football players to try out for the college football team as a punter. Having played lacrosse at a prep school in Baltimore, nationally renowned for its lacrosse program, I was offered and accepted the job to be the Assistant Coach for the lacrosse team at Gettysburg College my first year of seminary as well, and played club lacrosse for several years after graduating from seminary. So athletic competition has always been a part of my life and continues to be to this very day.

In the fall of the year, each seminary class fielded a football team. From those respective teams, an all-star team was chosen to compete against the students from the Lutheran Theological Seminary in Philadelphia. Consequently, my first football practice with my class team was special for me. It provided me with something familiar – solid ground on which I could stand with my peers. I met several married students who had been college football players. I met single students who shared my love of sports and competition. As it turned, out there were quite a few exceptional athletes in my class, and it showed on the field! Our quarterback had been the captain of his college team. Two of our linebackers had played in college as well. The class just ahead of us was also well manned by good athletes, but our class was something special. As a wide receiver, I caught passes from someone who could really throw a football, and at the end of the season we were both chosen to play against the team from Philadelphia. In that game we teamed up again for a victory the whole campus celebrated that evening.

As a result, some of the barriers I had been feeling, whether real or self-imposed, had been broken down. At last I felt a part of something, and although I would never be collegial with every one of my fellow students in terms of what we believed and understood, I could be one of them and share with them in a mutual acceptance of our differences.

In all honesty, those early days at Gettysburg had been uncomfortable for me, and I wondered, for a time, if I was doing the right thing. Did God really want me to serve Him as a Pastor when I found myself feeling so different about so many things from those who were there with me?

God then gave me the release I needed. Through sports He gave me a gift that enabled me to feel as if I belonged. And yet that wasn't the greatest gift He gave me that year. It was several months later before God really spoke to me and made me even more aware of the truth that He puts us exactly where He wants us and needs us to be.

First year seminarians in the Lutheran Church are required to apply for a quarter of what is generally known as CPE, which is an acronym for Clinical Pastoral Education. That requirement is usually fulfilled during the summer after the conclusion of the first year of academic work. However, it is during the year that applications have to be submitted, and there are an extraordinary number of opportunities from which to choose. Clinical Pastoral Education programs are offered in hospitals, prisons, and psychiatric hospitals throughout the country. The choice, therefore, isn't always about the program but more specifically the locale. If you are studying on the East Coast, you may want to spend a summer on the West Coast or vice versa. The choices are many and varied.

My desire was to stay close to home. My parents had bought a house on the water, and I enjoyed the boating and water-skiing that were available to me there in the summer and had no desire to go anywhere else. So I applied to a psychiatric hospital in Baltimore County, as did my roommate.

Much to my surprise, however, I received an acceptance letter from the CPE supervisor at a hospital near Annapolis. It was a place I had never heard of before, even though I had spent most of my life in Maryland, but it was closer to home, and with my plans for a summer full of fun on the water, I wasn't about to complain.

As it turned out, the supervisor who contacted me had been on the staff of the hospital to which I had originally applied. He had left there to become the chaplain and CPE supervisor at the hospital to which I was accepted. As he strove to develop the CPE program at this new location, he discovered that the hospital would be unable to provide housing for the students he hoped to bring into his program. Consequently, he needed to accept students who had housing available to them in the area or who could commute from where they were living while attending seminary. Having seen my application to the program he was about to leave, and realizing that my address of record was close to the hospital to which he was going, he took my application with him, and I became one of his students.

Early in June of 1970, I arrived for my first day as a student in the Clinical Pastoral Education Program at Crownsville State Hospital near Annapolis, Maryland. I was one of two Lutherans in the program. The other was a married classmate of mine from Gettysburg, who was a second career seminarian, which means that he had worked in another profession before entering seminary. The rest were students from the Episcopal Seminary in Washington, D.C., and all of them were older and married as well.

On the first day we were divided into two groups. My supervisor was the one who had accepted me into the program and who was actually in charge of the program. He was a Baptist minister who loved to fish and was fun to be around. Though his theology was different from mine and from the majority of the students, from what I remember, I liked him and enjoyed working with him.

We were each assigned to different areas of the hospital. I was responsible for two wards of men who were confined to a specific area, due to their various stages of mental illness, and to a ward of women, who were not only mentally impaired but physically challenged as well.

Ministry, in such a setting, can best be described as a "ministry of presence." The sight of someone wearing a clerical collar walking among the patients was often enough. Just to let them know that someone cared was important, especially when that someone could be identified as a representative of God and His Church. There were, of course, patients with whom you could converse, and that was important since verbatims, that is word for word transcriptions of our counseling sessions with the patients, needed to be prepared and presented to our supervisors.

On Sundays we were scheduled to conduct worship services in the hospital's gymnasium, which was a different worship experience than any I had ever known. The patients' behavior was unpredictable in this environment. Some would shout out various comments during the sermon. One would spend his time working over the punching bag that hung from the gym wall. Others would be out of their seats and moving around. It was definitely not a normal Lutheran worship setting, but it did serve to prepare the worship leader to be ready for anything, which does indeed come in handy.

All in all, it was an interesting summer, especially since it provided another kind of experience for me, which changed my life forever, and made me realize again how God's hand is so often present in our lives and the direction they take.

Another group of students was at Crownsville that summer. They had been sent from Peninsula General Hospital in Salisbury, Maryland, and had just finished their first year of nursing school. For them, the hospital had provided housing, but as a class, they had been divided. The married members of the class had been sent to a hospital closer to their homes, allowing them to commute and remain with their families, and the single students were assigned to Crownsville. It was there that they would be receiving their required quarter of Psychiatric Nurses Training.

Naturally, being the only single chaplain around, the presence of the nursing students piqued my interest. I would see them at lunch in the cafeteria with their white uniforms and caps, but they never came to the part of the hospital to which I had been assigned. (I was to learn later that it was considered too dangerous of an area for them to visit.) We would speak in passing at lunch, from time to time, but I really never had the opportunity during the day to make my way to their part of the hospital or to see them socially after hours.

One afternoon, while walking with another chaplain, I saw a softball game being played on one of the hospital's fields. We stopped to watch for a while and saw that the nurses were playing ball with the patients. It was quite a spectacle. The nurses were all in white on a dusty field, and the patients were running and skipping and having a grand time. While watching the game, I noticed the ball being hit to third base, and a nurse caught it in the fold of her skirt. As I watched her, I became immediately enamored. She was extremely pretty with short, dark hair, and having made that catch, she seemed quite athletic as well. I observed her for a while, since I found it hard not to, and eventually remarked to my fellow chaplain how pretty she was.

It just so happened that our supervisor had planned a party for us later that week, and I didn't have a date. I had been out of the area for over five years by then, since I had gone to college in North Carolina and seminary in Pennsylvania, and had really lost touch with all of my old friends from home. Fortunately for me, however, the other chaplain had the answer. His assigned area happened to be one of the places where the student nurses worked, and he told me if I stopped by to see him later that day, he would arrange to introduce me to the "third basemen" who had caught my eye. I couldn't wait, and he was certainly true to his word.

Later that afternoon, I was introduced to Nancy Jenkins. Unfortunately, she had plans for the weekend of our planned chaplain's party, so I went alone. But, I could not stop thinking about her.

The following week my sister and brother-in-law were flying in from a vacation in Puerto Rico, and I was supposed to pick them up at the airport after work. I asked Nancy if she would like to go with me, and she agreed. So we left the hospital and drove to the airport in Baltimore. We enjoyed talking and learning more about each other, and all in all it was a great day.

Much to my surprise, however, my parents had decided to welcome my sister and her husband home as well, so we ran into them at the airport. I couldn't imagine what Nancy must have been thinking. Not only was she getting to know me for the first time, but suddenly she was also meeting my whole family. She handled it gracefully, however, and was immediately made to feel comfortable and welcome by all. So when my mother invited us back to the house on the water for dinner – something she said she would just throw together – we all agreed.

The "thrown together" dinner was a hit. My mother never just threw things together. She was an excellent cook, so we had shish-kabobs on the grill and all kinds of other dishes to enjoy. Nancy was made to feel at home, and everyone liked her. It was the beginning of something so very special.

Shortly thereafter, we had our first real date to a movie. Later in the summer, we went with some friends of mine to an Oriole baseball game. As a result of my friend's connections, we had great seats in the first row, right behind the catcher.

Nancy and I were inseparable that summer. We ate lunch together nearly every day and went out after work. We spent the weekends at my parent's house on the water and went boating and swimming. I soon went down to the Eastern Shore of Maryland to meet her family. The summer flew by, and it was fun.

Time to go back to school came all too quickly. Nancy would return to Salisbury and to her nursing studies, and I would go back to the seminary in Gettysburg. Our time together from that moment on would be limited. But we had come to realize, by the end of that summer, that we were meant to be together and to remain so forever.

The week after school started, Nancy got a ride with another nursing student to a town just across the Chesapeake Bay Bridge from Annapolis. I came down from seminary and picked her up there to spend the weekend at my parents' house. Before going home, however, I took her to a scenic overlook from which you could look across the Severn River to the U.S. Naval Academy. There I proposed to her and gave her a ring, which was a family heirloom I had taken to have reset for her.

Nancy graduated from nursing school on 15 August 1971 and on 21 August 1971 we were married in a little Presbyterian church in her home town of Princess Anne, Maryland, by her Presbyterian pastor and my brother-in-law, who was a Lutheran pastor.

If I had not gone to Crownsville for CPE, and if the CPE supervisor who chose me for that program had not been hired to be the chaplain there, and if Nancy had been assigned to another hospital, as were some of her classmates, our paths would never have crossed. I had no intention of going to Crownsville. I didn't even know Crownsville existed, since it didn't even have a CPE program of record before I went there. It all just happened, and it was all out of my control.

When I reflect on these series of events, the only conclusion I can draw is that God's hand was at work in all that occurred. It was God who wanted me in Crownsville that summer. It was God who put Nancy there as well. It was God who brought us together. And my life has truly been blessed as a result. Indeed, God is at work in our lives. We just have to take the time to reflect on where we have been and what we have experienced in order to realize that God is with us. To follow His lead is to experience His blessings.

CHAPTER 3

A Positive Change Of Course

At the conclusion of the second year of academic requirements, a Lutheran seminarian enters into a period of training known as "the internship." It provides each prospective candidate for ordination the opportunity to put theory into practice. Each candidate is basically "farmed out" for approximately one year to work in a parish setting under the watchful eye and diligent guidance of an experienced pastor. For many it is a make or break experience, and whereas the majority of the candidates do well and move on, there is a percentage from each class who discover, as a result of their internship, that the ministry is not for them.

The opportunities available for internships are wide and varied. Some choose to work within English-speaking congregations overseas. I had friends who went to London and Tokyo, as well as the Caribbean Islands. Most, however, tend to remain within the continental United States, and that was certainly my choice.

In fact, I had known since entering seminary exactly where I wanted to go for my internship year, and for that I had my brother-in-law to thank. It just so happened that as I was preparing to enter seminary, he was preparing to conclude his internship in Bridgeport, Connecticut. Good brother-in-law that I am, I went to visit my sister and her husband in the waning days of their time in Bridgeport to help them with their move back to Gettysburg, Pennsylvania, for their final year of seminary.

Consequently, I had the opportunity to meet the pastor who had been his supervisor and to become acquainted with the church where he had served as an intern. The whole setting reminded me of my home church. Located in a suburban area, with a white collar and well-educated congregation, it had wonderful facilities and a large membership.

My brother-in-law had obviously enjoyed his time there and had grown extremely close to his supervisor and the congregation in general. I sensed his sorrow upon having to preach his final sermon as an intern and the congregation's reluctance to say farewell.

I knew right away that was where I wanted to be when the time came, and figured that with my brother-in-law's connections, I would one day be having the wonderful experience in Bridgeport, Connecticut, that he had apparently so enjoyed.

As my second year of seminary progressed, I found myself extremely busy with a variety of demands and expectations relative to my time and energy: the required academic course load, the wedding plans to be made with Nancy, my job at Gettysburg College as the Assistant Varsity Lacrosse Coach, and the jockeying for positions and the politicking that was often required to obtain internship positions. It was a lot to handle, but throughout my life I had learned to be adept at multi-tasking, and I never felt overwhelmed.

What I learned as things developed, however, was that the internship in Bridgeport, Connecticut, I so desired was something of a "plum." It had a wonderful reputation and was a site several others were considering, with the leading candidate, according to campus scuttlebutt, being the president of my class who was from New England. I knew him well, since our class was small and I was its vice-president, and I was cognizant of his capabilities. I, therefore, began to resign myself to the fact that I had better be ready to head elsewhere. Still, I listed Bridgeport as my first choice and trusted that God would send me to the right place – hoping, of course, that God's will and mine at that point were synonymous.

As things turned out, God and I appeared to be on the same page. Even the Director of Field Education at the seminary (the person responsible for placing seminarians in internship settings) seemed more than a bit surprised when he called me to his office to inform me of my placement. The pastor in Bridgeport, after reviewing the applicants, had requested me.

Naturally, I was thrilled. It is what I had been thinking about for the first two years of my seminary experience. It is where I wanted to be with Nancy as we began our life together. It was, from my perspective, the perfect place to be an intern, and it appeared as if my plans were coming together just as I had hoped.

The last few months of my second year in seminary went by quickly. My coaching job at the college paid me $600 for the season, and that was enough to enable me to work with a travel agent in Gettysburg to plan a honeymoon to Bermuda. Nancy was finishing nursing school and was to graduate on 15 August. Less than a week later, on 21 August, we were to be married.

With all of those plans coming together, we had the additional demand, now that we would be spending a year in Connecticut, of making arrangements to move some of our personal belongings to New England, so that I would be ready to start my work at the church as soon as we returned from Bermuda.

Fortunately, the intern preceding me there was a good friend. He and his wife were living in the apartment the church maintained for its interns and welcomed us to send some of our things ahead. They would store them for us and make sure everything was prepared for our arrival. At the same time, Nancy began to get in touch with hospitals in the Bridgeport area in order to secure employment. It was an exciting time for us. Things were going as planned and we were happy.

Then, just a few weeks before our wedding date, I received a call from the seminary's Director of Field Education. "I need to talk to you," he said. "The pastor you were to work with in Bridgeport has notified us that he doesn't think he will be able to have an intern this year, and we have to find you another placement."

It was shattering news. By that time, Nancy had received a job offer in Bridgeport, we had already forwarded some of our personal items to our new address there, and we had done everything possible to make our transition go as smoothly as possible. Now we found ourselves in the position of having to start all over, and the wedding was just a few weeks away.

Shocked and disappointed, I drove to the seminary and met with the Director of Field Education. "There are only two possibilities available to you," he said. "One is in Springfield, Massachusetts, and the other is in Smithsburg, Maryland.

The church in Massachusetts was apparently comparable to the one in Bridgeport. It was a large, suburban congregation with a lot to offer. But, for some reason, I had suddenly soured on the idea of spending time in New England. I had the feeling there was nothing there for me and experienced no sense of excited anticipation as I considered what was being offered.

As a native of Maryland, however, I had never heard of Smithsburg and had no idea where it was. Nevertheless, I found myself making a quick, and, perhaps, on the surface, a rather rash decision that I was going to stay in Maryland, no matter what, so I studied the congregational profile that was handed to me.

Part of the then Maryland Synod of the Lutheran Church in America St. Paul Lutheran Church in Greensburg, Maryland, and Mt. Moriah Lutherah Church in Foxville, Maryland, were both located just outside of Smithsburg. Together they comprised a two-church parish and each congregation was struggling to stay alive. The calling of a full-time ordained pastor was financially out of the question, and with a thriving and larger LCA congregation, Trinity Lutheran in Smithsburg close by, the Synod was considering the viability of keeping the two smaller churches open.

As I came to understand the process, it was at this point in the Synod's deliberations that the Seminary's internship program came into play. If the two congregations could handle the yearly stipend for an intern (which is quite minimal), and if the pastor of Trinity Lutheran would agree to be the intern supervisor, the intern could assume the duties of a pastor and, hopefully, help the congregations begin to grow and prosper with the goal being to call an ordained pastor.

The setting for these two congregations was rural. I was a city boy with no knowledge of or experience with life in a rural setting, aside from what I had learned from singing "Old MacDonald Had a Farm." Sure, I had been to a farm for a visit, from time to time but really didn't know a lot about the day to day workings of a farm, or what it was like to live full time in such a community.

Nancy, on the other hand, came from a somewhat rural area on the Eastern Shore of Maryland, so she was certainly more in tune with such things than I and perhaps more comfortable than she would have been in a suburban New England setting. This realization served to support the decision I had already made, and so my commitment to the internship at what I came to call the Foxville-Greensburg Lutheran Parish was complete.

The only problem was we had no place to live. A late entry into the race for interns, those responsible for putting the plan into action in an attempt to save the two congregations I would be serving had not secured housing should an intern become available. When the word reached the churches that I would be the intern, I was invited to meet with representatives from the two congregations to discuss, in detail, the arrangements for our arrival.

The meeting was pleasant and the people were nice, but the bottom line was that they had no place for us to live. We were closer than ever to our wedding day and to the start of my internship, so this predicament was quite a concern for us, as anyone might imagine.

The result of the meeting was that the congregations were going to look into buying a mobile home and placing it on a piece of ground next to an old, historic school building that belonged to Mt. Moriah. They showed me the brochures they had gathered on mobile homes and pointed out the one they hoped to purchase for our use. Nothing was definite, however, since permits would probably be needed, as well as sewer, water, and electric hook-ups. In other words, there was a lot to be done and little time to accomplish the task before our arrival. But, I was encouraged by the words of the committee chair who said, "Don't let this bother you! Focus on your wedding day, have a wonderful honeymoon, and we'll have things ready for you when you return."

I had no choice but to have faith that everything would work out for the best, even though on the drive back home, I kept wondering how Nancy would react to the apparent uncertainty of our situation when I called to share what I had just heard.

On August 15, 1971, Nancy graduated from nursing school, and the following Saturday, as planned, we were married. We took our honeymoon to Bermuda and, upon our return, began to pack for our move to Smithsburg.

During our week away, we couldn't help but wonder what we would be facing when we got home. Had housing been obtained for us? Would my internship be delayed in some way if housing was still unavailable? Or had the people I would be shepherding as an intern come up with a plan?

As soon as we returned from Bermuda, I called my contact in Smithsburg and was invited to bring Nancy for a visit to our new home. The two congregations had found a house for us in the little town of Smithsburg – a big, two story, older, but beautiful house with a wrap-around porch, three bedrooms, and two baths. We were ecstatic and anxious to move in and get started.

I was soon to discover that this internship would be different than any I had ever heard of before. The Bishop of the Maryland Synod gave me a letter authorizing me to celebrate the sacraments – something not usually done by someone yet to be ordained.

The reason for this special privilege was that I was going to be acting more as a pastor than as an intern. On Sunday mornings I would be preaching at two different churches every week, whereas most interns may preach only once a month. On the Sunday when communion was to be celebrated, I would be the one presiding at worship and, therefore, the only celebrant available. When a child was to be baptized, once again, I was the only one available on Sunday mornings to celebrate the baptism.

It was a unique and wonderful opportunity for an intern. My supervisor had a church of his own to care for, and was not with me on Sunday mornings to evaluate my handling of the worship services and to hear my preaching. Consequently, he had to rely on the input he received from the members of the congregations I was serving, and fortunately, the feedback was positive.

We would meet frequently during the week to discuss my progress, development, and any concerns I might have, or questions I might need to ask, but basically I was a pastor. I led all the committee meetings for two separate congregations. I presided at the Church Council meetings. I did all the shut-in visits, hospital calls, and counseling.

Smithsburg wasn't Bridgeport, and the two congregations I served were not large and wealthy. But they were rich in so many other ways and for me, so was the entire experience. I grew to love those people, that area, and being a pastor.

Nancy and I had a wonderful time there, and our first year of marriage and my internship progressed all too rapidly. As the year drew near to a close, and we anticipated our return to seminary for my final year, we had severely ambivalent feelings. We didn't want to leave our friends and our church families. And they didn't want us to go either.

An effort was made to pave the way for our return, upon my graduation from Gettysburg Seminary, to become the full-time, ordained pastor they were hoping for. But the Synod office was not in favor of that plan.

I was to learn that the class behind me, having heard of my unique internship experience, was enthralled by the opportunity to follow in my footsteps. I could certainly understand why! It was a special opportunity any seminarian would be thrilled to have, and though I wasn't looking forward to giving it up, I could never deny someone else the chance to experience, as an intern, what I had experienced.

When we learned who my successor was to be, Nancy and I invited him and his wife for dinner one night to see the house and to share thoughts about what their year would be like.

Our going away party was a real joy. Not only was it a celebration of our year together, and the friendships we had formed, but it was also a celebration of the first anniversary of our marriage. It was a surprise party held in a barn with a fun-filled, country re-enactment of our wedding. We laughed, shared memories of the things we had done together, and even shed a tear or two as we said our farewells. We have never forgotten the people of St. Paul's and Mt. Moriah and never will.

After having three interns, the Foxville-Greensburg Lutheran Parish was able to call their own ordained pastor, and now some forty years later are going strong. The internship program was a blessing to the parish, as the parish was a blessing to its interns.

When I was selected to become the intern at the church in Bridgeport, I felt as if God and I were on the same page. It was where I wanted or believed I needed to be, and when word came that it had worked out as I had hoped, I took that to be God's affirmation of my desire.

Obviously, however, God had other plans. Once again He took control of my life and gave me a change of course that put me on a much more positive and constructive track. As an introvert, I needed the opportunity to be in a position where I had to be more assertive, more responsible, more comfortable when on center stage, and more confident in myself and in my abilities! If I were to have any chance at all to be successful as a parish pastor, I had to have an experience that would give me the greatest opportunity available to develop in that role.

A normal internship would not have done that for me. Only something unique, like the situation in Smithsburg, could provide it and God gave me that opportunity. God created for me exactly what I needed. God changed the course that I had set and led me to sail the course I truly needed to sail.

God **does** know what is best for us, and He **does** what is best for us! We may not always acknowledge His active presence in our lives, or the "burning bush" experiences we might have, but God is with us and so are those experiences!

CHAPTER 4

Where To Begin

The last year of seminary is an incredibly hectic and often unnerving experience. Not only are there academic requirements to complete, but there is also the drama, and for some the trauma, associated with what is known as the "call process" – the series of examinations and interviews that lead to a seminarian's call or hiring by his or her first congregation. Without that call a seminarian may well graduate but will not be ordained! So the pressure is there to be accepted by a congregation looking for someone to fill its pastoral vacancy.

Moving back to Gettysburg, Pennsylvania, following my internship year, was special for Nancy and me. It was to be her first experience living there and sharing in all of the activities of the seminary community, and that was something to which we were looking forward.

We were able to rent the very same apartment that my sister and brother-in-law used during their last year in Gettysburg. It was only a block from the campus, so I could walk or bike to school, while Nancy took the car to work. She had been hired as a nurse at the Lutheran Home in Gettysburg, and consequently became the "bread winner" for us, while I finished my required courses.

Gettysburg is such a special and lovely place. In spite of the horror that once occurred there during the Civil War, it remains a picturesque and historic little town in a delightfully bucolic setting. We loved our time there and filled it with evening bike rides on the battlefield, walks through town, and visits to the nearby apple festivals and other events for which the area was known.

Overshadowing those good times, however, was the reality that the time was at hand for me not only to be approved by my Synod for ordination, but also to be selected by a congregation as its pastor, so I could be ordained. For me and my classmates, it was to be a year of anxious uncertainty.

The fall went by quickly. My classes were interesting, and my grades were good. It wasn't until after the Christmas break that things would begin to change and get a lot more serious.

Early in 1973, I received an announcement from the Examining Committee of what was at that time the Maryland Synod of the Lutheran Church in America. (In the mid-1980's a merger with two other Lutheran groups led to the creation of what is now the Delaware-Maryland Synod of the Evangelical Lutheran Church in America.) This was my home Synod, and I was required after three years of theoretical and practical preparation for the ordained ministry to be examined by them so that they might determine my fitness for the ministry. Needless to say, this stands as a nerve racking experience for any seminarian, and I was no exception.

On the evening assigned, I reported to the Synod office in Baltimore, Maryland. Nancy and my parents dropped me off with hugs and good wishes and then went for a drive to deal with their own nerves while I stood outside the Synod office building in the dark waiting for my appointed hour to arrive.

The committee, however, was late. Having completed the afternoon examinations, the committee members had gone out for dinner and were more than a little tardy returning. I, of course, was unaware of the reason for their delayed return, and in the days prior to cell phones they were unable to contact me with the information that would have alleviated my concern. So, since the Synod office was locked and no one was around, I could only stand as patiently as possible outside the place in which my future would be determined at some point that night and wonder when those who held that future in their hands would finally arrive.

Eventually the committee members did make their way back, and my anxiously awaited examination began. As requested, I had submitted copies of my sermons to them, as well as some other required written materials. They also, if my memory is correct, had copies of my intern supervisor's evaluation and other such documents deemed pertinent for the success of the task that was theirs to perform.

Questions relative to my theology and my proclamation of the Gospel were asked, as well as inquiries relative to my understanding of and approach to the ordained ministry of the Lutheran Church. I felt comfortable with my responses and confident that the experience was going well.

One of the examiners then began to offer a series of questions related to how I would handle conflict within a congregation. His approach was so aggressive that had I been testifying in a courtroom, I would have hoped that my attorney would object on the grounds that the prosecutor was "badgering the witness." I began to feel cornered and uncertain and anxious about my responses.

In retrospect, I believe I floundered at this point because I had never experienced conflict within a congregation as a pastor. I had heard stories from my parents about congregational meetings that had gotten so heated they had to be adjourned and moved to another location because it was felt that the comments being voiced were being expressed in language inappropriate for the sanctuary. But I had never been a part of such a thing.

The truth is, I had never really had much conflict in my life at all. I was blessed with wonderful, loving parents who were devoted to one another and to their children. I had a supportive sister who attended the games I played as an athlete and encouraged me in other ways as well. And, I had lots of friends in school, who remain my friends to this day; therefore, I was not experienced when it came to dealing with conflict. Even my internship, the only setting where I might have had conflict to deal with as a "pastor" in training, was anything but contentious.

Consequently, I was lost. I had no good answers to give to what I began to consider my "antagonist" and as a result came to the conclusion that I was in conflict with him. Unfortunately, he was good at it – obviously experienced with it – and I was not. It made me aware that maybe I had a lot more to learn and that thought led me to the conclusion that I had failed. I would not be approved for ordination. I would not become the pastor of a church.

Finally, the examination concluded, and I was excused. I was told to wait while the committee deliberated and made its decision. It was a seemingly endless and painful experience of solitude filled with dreadful misgivings.

After what seemed like a lifetime, I was asked to return to the room and face the committee's judgment. God, who had called me through a small cross embedded in the bark of a tree to the Gospel ministry, confirmed that call for me that night when the chairperson of the examining committee related to me, with a smile, that I had been approved for ordination.

What a relief! What a joy! What a blessing! I thanked them sincerely, and as I left the room, eager to tell Nancy and my parents the good news, several of the members of the committee approached me to express their dismay about how the whole issue, relative to conflict, had been handled by one of their own. They assured me that what was most important was my understanding of Lutheran theology and my obvious feeling for the ministry. I appreciated their sentiments and their encouragement and thanked God for their understanding.

I have come to the, perhaps, simplistic realization over the years since that night that if you understand that a pastor's calling is to share the good news of God's grace and love in every way possible with those you are called to serve and care for them as a good shepherd cares for his sheep with kindness, tenderness, and sincere concern for their well-being, conflict will not raise its ugly head within a congregation.

After that night I served as a parish pastor for thirty-six years, went through three major building programs, and made changes in worship and other parish life experiences, and I cannot remember one significant conflict that threatened to destroy a congregation or its relationship with its pastor. Perhaps that is an anomaly. I would rather think of it as a ratification of the sentiments expressed by those members of my examining committee who emphasized the importance of understanding what you believe, being able to communicate it as best you can through words and deeds, and striving at all times to follow the example of "the Good Shepherd" – Jesus Christ – who calls us to follow and serve.

Those reflections, however, come at the conclusion of the journey that began for me the night I was approved for ordination. My next step after that night was to find a church that wanted me so my journey could continue, and that step is referred to as "getting a call."

It began when an assistant to the Bishop met with me to discuss my options. Did I want a church of my own? Did I want to be part of a staff? Did I want an urban, suburban, or a rural setting?

Since I had grown up on the west side of Baltimore, I knew what it was like to live in a city. And since I had attended a church in a suburban setting, I was also familiar with the suburbs. And since I had interned in a rural area, such a setting was not unfamiliar to me either. Consequently, it really didn't matter. I just wanted a call. Still, I had to make a decision, and the first decision I made led to a great disappointment.

St. Martin's Lutheran Church in Annapolis, Maryland, was looking for an assistant pastor. My home wasn't far from Annapolis, and I loved the area. Nancy and I had met near Annapolis and had spent a great deal of time there while dating, so it was a special place for us both. Consequently, the thought of beginning my ministry there was exciting, and I opted to have St. Martin's as my first choice for a "call."

Unfortunately, I wasn't to be that congregation's first choice. They selected one of my classmates and friends instead, and I was crushed. Rejection isn't easy to endure, especially when your hopes are so high.

In the wake of that experience, I was offered a two-church parish in western Maryland, close to where I had interned. I would be the only pastor there, which was fine with me, but I was concerned, nonetheless. I had learned as an intern that in a two church parish you are usually leading worship at one church while the other church is having Sunday school. Then when you leave the first church, the Sunday school program begins there and is conducted while you are leading worship at the second church. Consequently, you are never involved as a pastor in Christian education on Sunday mornings, and that is something I didn't want to miss. I, therefore, decided not to be interviewed.

The next offer was to be considered for the position of assistant pastor at St. Mark's Lutheran Church in Hagerstown, Maryland, and I accepted. The interview went well, and I got the call. The excitement of that moment, the realization that graduation from seminary was at hand and my ordination assured, alleviated any remaining disappointment I felt as a result of my rejection in Annapolis. I was ready to begin my ministry. I was ready to be the Rev. William F. R. Gilroy, and to be called "Pastor."

On May 27, 1973, at Second English Lutheran Church (my home congregation) in Baltimore, Pastor Augustus Hackmann, who had helped guide me to that moment, presented me to Bishop Paul Orso, as my family and friends watched. With the laying on of hands, the pronouncement of the appropriate words, and the placing of the stole, which is symbolic of a pastor's office, I was ordained a Minister of the Church of Christ in the Office of the Word and Sacraments according to the Confession and Order of the Lutheran Church in America.

It was a special moment I will never forget.

After a few days off, I reported to St. Mark's Lutheran Church in Hagerstown, Maryland. Nancy and I had been able to purchase a little brick ranch house in the area with the help of some money we had saved for a down payment. It had just been built, and we were thrilled to have a home of our own.

My specific duties as the assistant pastor related to youth ministry and Christian education. I was also to share, with the senior pastor, the hospital and home visitations that are so important and accept other duties and responsibilities as he deemed appropriate.

The congregation welcomed Nancy and me warmly and made us feel very much at home. We made friends quickly and were happy with our new life in Hagerstown.

I did, however, have a lot to learn. Most internships basically provide a staff experience. In other words, as an intern, you are essentially a part of a church staff, and as such, you work directly under the supervision of a senior pastor. My internship had been different. I was on my own and was responsible for two different congregations. I had a supervisor, but he had his own church, and consequently, we were never together on Sunday mornings. And after a month or so of guidance, he allowed me to function as a pastor in terms of meeting with the appropriate committees, planning and goal setting, and administering the programs of both the congregations I was there to serve. So I was accustomed to working on my own and "doing my own thing."

But, I had accepted a call to be an assistant pastor and had to adapt to working as a team with the senior pastor of the congregation that had "hired" me. Personally we got along well. He was a fine man and a good pastor, but his approach to and philosophy relative to parish ministry was much different from mine.

As a result, some of my thoughts, proposals, and actions were often challenged. Since he was the senior pastor, he certainly was entitled to have the final say on what was being done, and I respected that. Still, it was difficult for me, at times, to feel somewhat restricted.

My internship had obviously spoiled me. I was accustomed to being on my own and not having someone else approve my actions and proposals. I had learned what worked in a parish and what didn't and was confident that I was a capable leader whose vision for a congregation was worthwhile and worth pursuing, and who understood how to get things done constructively.

Being part of a staff, therefore, was not always easy for me. It was, however, a learning experience. I can't help but believe that I grew as a result, and for that I am thankful. Later in my career, I would be called as the Senior Pastor to one of the largest Lutheran congregations in the Delaware-Maryland Synod of the ELCA with a staff of six, so the lessons learned in my early years in Hagerstown did, indeed, prove to be beneficial.

Reflecting on those early days, I can't help but think of one major event that changed the lives of some wonderful people in a special way. As part of the Youth Ministry program, I challenged the youth of St. Mark's to plan a trip to Disney World. It would be a year-long process involving fund raising, special activities that would involve the whole congregation, and the kind of bonding experiences that would make the group stronger.

The youth jumped at the challenge, and the work began. We held submarine sandwich sales, sponsored a Valentine Dance for the whole congregation, and planned our trip. We set dates, made the reservations, chartered a bus, took registrations, and determined how many chaperones would be needed.

By the time the day of departure arrived, the youth had raised enough money to substantially offset the cost of the trip. The total out-of-pocket expense per participant amounted to approximately $60. It was just amazing.

What was more amazing and exciting was that two of the chaperones were sisters, who had never been out of Hagerstown, and another was an elderly gentleman with no children or grandchildren involved, but who just wanted to go with us. For those three adults, this was the trip of a lifetime. Their joy and excitement was noticed by all, and even the youth were moved by the emotion of that experience. They were so encouraging and supportive of those adult chaperones, that as we boarded the bus at the end of the week to return home from Disney World, the older gentleman, with Mickey Mouse ears on his head, addressed that group of youngsters and offered his sincere thanks to them all for making him feel like one of them. It was a great experience for everyone involved and a highlight of my time at St. Mark's.

Eventually, however, my discomfort as an assistant, and my yearning for a church of my own led me to contact the Bishop and request consideration for another opportunity. I had been at St. Mark's for two and a half years by then, and had made some dear friends. Nancy and I were both reluctant to leave, but, it was time, and I trusted that the Holy Spirit would once more guide me in the right direction.

Called To Calvary

During my time in Hagerstown, I had gotten to know one of the assistants to the Bishop very well. We had formed a good friendship, and he was someone I could trust. So when I made it known that I was interested in leaving St. Mark's for another opportunity, he did something I considered a bit unusual. He submitted my name to two different congregations at the same time.

I had always understood that a pastor, seeking a new call, could only interview for one opening at a time. If that didn't work, then his or her name would be submitted to another congregation. Consequently, when the Bishop's assistant told me that he was submitting my name for two openings, I was a bit surprised, but also very thankful. It gave me the hope that my desire for a new challenge would be satisfied a little sooner than I might have imagined.

The first congregation to contact me for an interview was near Westminster, Maryland. The church was located in a rural area, which was rapidly becoming more of a suburban area, and had a lot to offer. The church itself was a beautiful red brick colonial style structure with a brick ranch style parsonage nearby. Ascetically, it was a locale very pleasing to the eye, and a place where I thought my family would be happy. The interview went well, I believed, and the prospects were exciting.

The second congregation was in the little town of Woodbine, Maryland. It was located in the southern end of Carroll County about 20-25 miles west of Baltimore. Unfortunately for me, however, the road I had to travel (U.S. Route 70) was undergoing some construction, and as a result, the exits were not clearly marked. Consequently, I missed the turn off for Woodbine on the day I was due there for my interview and drove approximately ten miles further before realizing my mistake.

Anxious already about the interview, I grew more and more dismayed as the time for my appointment drew near. First impressions mean so much, and the impression I was about to leave on that "call committee" would be one, I had convinced myself, of a person who was tardy and irresponsible.

Fortunately, that was not the case at all. Instead they were all very much aware of the confusion created by the road construction and had anticipated my problem, so my concerns were alleviated, and my reception was quite warm.

Unfortunately, **my** first impression of Woodbine itself was not the best. A hurricane had taken out the bridge that spanned the Patapsco River, and it was a bridge that had to be crossed to reach the church. The Army Corps of Engineers had erected a temporary span, which had become something of a permanent span, and it was a rickety, bumpy, uncertain structure over which one would pass with concern. Being a bit late and anxious, I hesitated only for a moment before committing myself and my car to such a passage, so I didn't think a whole lot about it at the time, I just went. Nancy, however, wasn't really comfortable with that decision but had no choice, so she closed her eyes and hung on. It was just one more hurdle on our journey that day, and thankfully, the bridge held.

The church itself was another disappointment. I had just interviewed with a congregation that offered a beautiful building and a parsonage to match. The church in Woodbine was an old frame structure in need of some work. There was no office for the pastor. The Sunday school rooms were located in the basement. The sanctuary was extremely small and the chancel was so narrow that I could stand in the middle and touch both the pulpit and the lectern at the same time. It did, however, have extremely beautiful stained glass windows.

The parsonage was also old and in need of remodeling – from the kitchen, to the worn carpeting, to the doors needing new locks, and the paint begging for a fresh coat.

The two interviews in terms of facilities being offered to a new pastor were reminiscent of a beauty and the beast scenario. One had everything going for it, and the other did not. But, as I came to realize and as the fairy tale portrays, there can be great beauty in the beast as well.

Again, the interview went well, and as the two churches considered me, I considered them. And once more the Lord spoke to me. The attractiveness of the first location called to me. It offered everything a young pastor could have hoped for. But that little voice I had learned to listen to kept speaking to me about Woodbine. It made me think about how comfortable I felt with the people there. It made me look beyond the obvious attractions being offered by the first congregation, so that I might see something even more attractive in the second. And when I did that, I came to the realization that the church really isn't a building. The church, as God desires us to define it, is the people of God gathered together as a fellowship of believers to worship and serve the Lord. And the more I thought about that, the more I began to see in the congregation at Woodbine a place where I could do some good, where my ministry would be truly special, and where Nancy and I could find a family that would welcome us warmly and love us dearly.

So I contacted the assistant to the Bishop, who was guiding me in my search for a new position, and told him I wanted to focus on Woodbine. I was convinced that was where God truly wanted me to be, and God confirmed that conviction by inspiring the congregation to extend to me the invitation to become its new pastor.

In February of 1976, I, therefore, tendered my resignation as the Assistant Pastor of St. Mark's Lutheran Church in Hagerstown, Maryland, and on 1 March 1976 I became the pastor of Calvary Lutheran Church in Woodbine, Maryland. Once more I was on my own.

I began my ministry in Woodbine during the season of Lent – one of the busiest and most hectic times of the church year. Until we were able to sell our house in Hagerstown, however, I commuted three days a week and worked from home the other two days. This was definitely a drawback, since I really wanted to be with my new congregation and community as much as possible, especially during Lent. But, I had to make the best of the situation.

Eventually, the house sold, and we moved to the parsonage beside the church in Woodbine. While I was commuting, the congregation had the time to remodel the kitchen, put down new carpeting, and paint the various rooms, so there was a bright side to my delayed move, and one Nancy and I really appreciated.

The only thing missing from the kitchen was a dishwasher – something Nancy insisted on having if she was going to move out of our new house in Hagerstown to the old remodeled parsonage in Woodbine – so I bought one for her. And with that our time in Hagerstown came to an end, and we embarked on our new journey together in Woodbine.

For the first nearly three years of my ministry, my focus had been on youth ministry and Christian education. Now, as the only pastor at Calvary Lutheran, I was responsible for everything relative to the congregation's life and well-being. I was the administrator, the counselor, the educator, the worship planner and leader, the visitor, the preacher, and the **shepherd.** It was an awesome position to be in, and one I relished. But, it was also one into which I had to grow.

Being a young pastor (I was only twenty-eight years old when I was called to Calvary) is often a detriment. Older members of any congregation, whose life experiences are more vast and varied, can find it difficult to come to someone so young for counsel and advice. I even had one member of Calvary come to me once to express that sentiment, and did so by telling me that, in his opinion, all seminarians should be "second career people", that is they should have more worldly experiences before entering the ministry.

Ironically, that is now true. The majority of those graduating from Lutheran seminaries today are more mature – often married and with children – and have come from other career fields. In my case, however, I entered seminary right out of college, as did the vast majority of my classmates, so I did not have a lot of life experiences to draw from. All I had was my determination to succeed and to be a good pastor. So I did the best I could with what I had, identified the weaknesses I needed to improve on, began to develop my own understanding of how to do God's will and work, and trusted God's continuing guidance.

One area of weakness I had begun to identify while in Hagerstown, and which is directly related, I believe, to a lack of experience, was pastoral counseling. Having had to deal with a member suffering from a severe emotional crisis during my time at St. Mark's, I had quickly come to the conclusion that seminary had not really prepared me to deal with such an issue. I was, however, able to get that person to someone more qualified, and having been invited to sit in on his session with this "client", I became both amazed and intrigued by his counseling skills.

Consequently, after moving to Woodbine, I visited with the Bishop one day to discuss my interest in becoming more qualified to do pastoral counseling. As an experienced counselor himself with a Ph.D. in that field, he was an excellent resource for me.

Fortuitously, (which for me is another way of saying that once again God took an active role in the direction my life would take) the Bishop had just been contacted by Loyola College (a Jesuit school) in Baltimore with the news that a Master of Science degree program in Pastoral Counseling was being opened at the college, and the school was looking for prospective candidates for the first class.

The Bishop recommended me that day, and an interview was scheduled with the program's director. I was impressed with what I learned about the program, excited about the possibility of continuing my education – especially as it related to my ministry – and I was accepted.

I did, of course, have to take this to my congregation, since it would mean time away from the parish if I were to return to school. And not only did I receive the approval I needed to enter the program but also the funding I would need, since the congregation established a continuing education fund for me, which covered my expenses. **God does indeed provide!**

For the next two years I was back in school. Fortunately, the program was set up with the understanding that most of the students were pastors, priests, and rabbis with full time congregational responsibilities. That being a given, the classes I took were always on Wednesdays and ran from 2 p.m. until approximately 10 p.m. It made for a long day, but it really helped with my schedule to know that only one day a week would need to be committed to the program aside, of course, from the preparation required outside of the classroom.

The courses were interesting and stimulating, and the practical application of what I had learned increased my competence as a counselor. I grew into the role as I had hoped and gained what I believed to be a certain expertise as a counselor, which served me well throughout my ministry.

In June of 1978, I received my degree and accepted an offer to do some part-time marriage and family counseling for a pastoral counseling clinic in Catonsville, Maryland.

During that time, things at Calvary were also going well. The congregation began to grow, Nancy was working part-time at a hospital, and my parents even moved into the area and became members of the church. It was a wonderful time for all of us. We felt the love of the congregation for the entire Gilroy family and returned that love wholeheartedly.

As a pastor, I shared the joys and sorrows of the people I had been called to shepherd, and grew to know how very important it is for a pastor to be present for his/her people. The "ministry of presence" is something truly special, and yet something not all pastors understand.

Again, God's hand guided me to this realization. One day, while I was still in Hagerstown, I had made a lot of visits. It was a hot, summer day, and it was late in the afternoon. I had convinced myself that I had done enough for one day, and I was tired and ready to head home. As I turned the car in that direction, however, I had a nagging feeling that there was one other visit I needed to make. It was someone I had on my list for that afternoon, but someone I believed I could put off until another time. So I struggled with the ambivalence I was feeling. Should I stop or shouldn't I? Could I wait for another day, or did I need to go to see that person immediately? It was quite a quandary for me!

But suddenly I realized that there was something stronger than my will compelling me to make that one additional visit. I began to understand that once more God was speaking to me and it was His will that I go and do what He obviously needed me to do. So I went to the home of an elderly widow who lived all alone.

What I didn't know prior to my visit was that she was having some health issues and had just undergone some tests. As we sat and talked that afternoon she shared her history with me, and it was obvious that she was quite concerned about what the test results might reveal – results that were due in that very day. She had been waiting for her doctor to call, and all day long her anxiety had grown. Being alone, she had no one to talk to, no one to share her concerns with, and the waiting had been extremely difficult. My presence there with her enabled her to vent, to express her feelings, to talk to someone, and not to feel so alone.

After I had been there for a while, the phone rang. It was her doctor. The results were in, and there was nothing seriously wrong with her. The relief was evident on her face as she hung up the phone. We rejoiced together and offered a prayer of thanksgiving together and as I left, she expressed to me how appreciative she was of my visit and how much it had meant to have someone there as she waited for that important call.

Of all the visits I had made that day, the last one was the most important, and yet it was one I almost failed to make. Consequently, I learned that day the importance of listening to God's still, small voice as it directs us to do His will. Throughout my ministry, I never second guessed that voice as it spoke to me from that moment on. I strove to be there for those entrusted to my care, to make every effort to let them know that I was going to be with them, no matter what, and that I cared about them. Whenever I felt that God needed me to be somewhere, that is where I was going to be, and the affirmation I was to receive time and time again relative to that determination was when I would hear the words, "Pastor, I knew you would be here!"

"The ministry of presence" is extremely important and something I believe God does indeed guide us to provide for one another. Personally, I know that striving to offer such a ministry enriched my life and gave it both meaning and purpose. It also enabled me to feel, in a special way, the nearness and direction of God.

As I continued the maturation process so important for all pastors, Calvary matured as well, and once again the Bishop offered me some advice, which I decided to take. Having just completed the degree in Pastoral Counseling, he encouraged me to enter a Doctor of Ministry program being offered jointly by the Lutheran Theological Seminary in Gettysburg and the one in Philadelphia. The Doctor of Ministry degree is a professional doctorate rather than an academic doctorate and is designed to make one more proficient in his or her ministry. Knowing of my desire to continue to develop as a pastor, he offered this directive, and so I applied to the program and was accepted.

In retrospect, I probably should have waited. It was not easy to move from one academic challenge to another, so having more time in between such endeavors probably would have been wise.

Besides, the congregation at Calvary had outgrown its old facility, and once again God had provided us with a great opportunity. The congregation inherited a substantial amount of money, and it was bequeathed with the understanding that it be used to build a whole new church. Consequently, the congregation had voted to enter into a building program, which required the purchase of property, the hiring of an architect, and all the other details relative to such a large construction project.

With all that going on, I really didn't need anything else on my plate, but I stuck to my decision to enroll in the doctoral program, confident that I could juggle everything successfully. Apparently, as someone once said, I love a challenge and tend to rise to the occasion. I don't know if that is exactly true, but I had certainly put myself in a position to prove it.

In 1978, as Calvary drew close to a major construction project, I began to work on my doctorate. Two years later, as if there wasn't enough to keep me busy already, my thoughts turned once more to the possibility of becoming a Navy chaplain.

By that time I was the father of two sons. I loved my family dearly and no longer harbored any desire to go on active duty, as I had envisioned during my days in seminary, since it would mean extended separations from them. But I did start thinking about the reserve program and what it had to offer in terms of allowing me to serve my country and minister to the men and women of our uniformed services.

My first hurdle was Nancy. She was far from thrilled by the prospect, and I appreciated her concern. But one of my closest friends in the ministry had been in the Army reserve as a chaplain for many years, and having him as a consultant was a great help. So, with Nancy's reticent approval, I began to do some research and made the appropriate connections. As a result, I was commissioned as a LTJG in the U.S. Navy Chaplain Corps in March of 1980, and attended the first half of the Basic Course for Chaplains that summer at the Naval Education and Training Center in Newport, Rhode Island. My commitment was for two days a month and two weeks a year for training and active service, which my congregation once more approved.

It was an extremely busy time and a time when I was wearing a great many "hats"! I was a husband and father, a pastor responsible for a growing congregation in the midst of a significant building program, a student working on a doctorate, and a chaplain in the Navy. In retrospect, I am not sure how I handled all of that, or the wisdom I exhibited when getting involved in so many varied endeavors, but I truly feel as if God guided me to undertake those challenges and gave me the strength I needed to face them successfully.

In 1981, I finished the second half of the Basic Course for Chaplains and found myself well on the way to a very special, rewarding, and meaningful career in the Navy. Though it took me longer than I had hoped, as a result of my many commitments, I received the Doctor of Ministry degree in 1984, and later that year the new home for Calvary Lutheran Church was completed. I thank God for those accomplishments and cherish the memories they have given me. Together they contributed in significant ways to my development both as a pastor and as a person, and enabled me to truly realize in a special way that with God all things are possible.

Looking back on those days, the greatest challenge was probably the building program. And I say that because such an endeavor can often be both disruptive and divisive for a congregation. Again, however, God's presence and guidance was most evident.

The architect we hired was a fine Christian gentleman, active in his own Lutheran church, and a relative of one of Calvary's members. He did an excellent job designing Calvary's new church home, and even incorporated the beautiful windows from the old church into the construction of the new. The property we located for the project was acquired at a very reasonable price, and the contractor hired was easy to work with and, on top of everything, in a positive and expeditious way.

One member of Calvary played a special, though quiet role, in the success of the project. A humble yet popular figure, not only within the congregation but also throughout the county in which he lived, he had been diagnosed with cancer and fought a courageous battle against this dreaded disease. We prayed together a lot and went to a healing service together as well. His faith and courage were remarkable, and God was with him. Consequently, he weathered the storm and won the war. As a result, he felt as if

God had helped him continue to live for a time in order to see the new church built. He, therefore, contributed to the success of the project in many special ways.

One night, as the bequeathed funds were nearly exhausted, and we were facing the prospect of having to – for the first time – tap into the money the bank had agreed to loan us, I called him to relate that news. He told me he would be right over. A few minutes later he appeared at my door and sat with me for a time in my living room.

"Let's not touch the mortgage money just yet," he told me. "We can use this instead." And with that he took out his checkbook and wrote a check to the church for $10,000. It was the most incredible act of benevolent and faithful stewardship I had ever witnessed, and something I still remember vividly to this day.

Because of his efforts and the unbelievably creative, imaginative, and passionate support of the entire congregation for what we were attempting to accomplish together, a great deal of money was raised, the congregation grew stronger as a result of working so hard together to reach the goal we had set, and Calvary's new church home became a reality.

It was my first experience with a building program, but it would not be me last. I was to face at least three other major projects throughout the course of my ministry, and each one would be a challenge. The first one, however, seems to be the most memorable because it is the first.

During the construction of the church my life was once again disrupted by the intrusion of the Holy Spirit in a significant way. A new Bishop had been chosen to lead our Synod, and once he settled into his office, I arranged to meet with him to bring him up to date on the Woodbine congregation.

With the construction drawings in hand, I went to his office and excitedly told him about all that we were attempting to accomplish. An old friend with whom I had worked on several projects for the Synod, he politely listened to my presentation and expressed an appropriate interest. When I was finished, however, he had a question, and it was not about Calvary.

"How would you like to be considered for the position of Senior Pastor at St. John in Linthicum?" he asked, and I was astonished. St. John is the church he had served for twenty years prior to being elected Bishop. He was putting together a list of candidates to be considered by that congregation, and he wanted to add my name to that list.

I was shocked. I had not expressed an interest in leaving Calvary. I loved it there and was in the midst of a large building project. It was my home. The church was growing. There was more to do. But though my reticence was no doubt obvious to him and my sentiments sincere, he still said, "Bill, I think you would be a good fit at St. John." So, before I left, I gave him permission to enter my name for consideration. He was, after all, the Bishop. Besides, as I drove home considering all that had happened, I reached the conclusion that nothing would ever come of it anyway. St. John was one of the largest congregations in the Synod. I was only thirty-six years old, had been ordained just eleven years, and had been a senior pastor for only eight years. There were so many other candidates with much more experience, pastors who had paid their dues and were deserving of such a call, so I was sure that a church like St. John would have no interest in me, and I would continue at Calvary.

In June of 1984, I was contacted by the St. John search committee. I had just received my doctorate and the chairman of the committee was the first person to refer to me as Dr. Gilroy, which I admit sounded nice, even though I later told her and the other members of the committee I preferred to be called pastor. A meeting was scheduled and, within a week or two, I traveled to Linthicum, Maryland, for an interview.

No doubt because I had convinced myself from the beginning that a call to St. John was something I didn't believe to be feasible, I was more relaxed than usual for such a setting and enjoyed the discussion immensely. I felt as if I related well to all who were there and answered their questions appropriately and with good detailed responses. When I got home, Nancy asked how it went, and I said, "Great!" It was a good experience I told her, and I was glad I had gone, but I really didn't expect to hear from them anymore.

Not long after that meeting, I left for two weeks of active duty as a Navy Chaplain. My orders were to relieve the protestant chaplain at the Naval Air Station in Bermuda, so that he could take two weeks leave with his family back in the States. I had spoken with him on the phone in preparation for my time there, and he extended to me the invitation to use his house while he was away and to bring my family. So while I worked, Nancy and the boys enjoyed two weeks on the beautiful island of Bermuda, and we all had a wonderful time.

Shortly after returning home, I received a surprise. The chairperson of the St. John pastoral search committee contacted me and requested another meeting, and this time they invited Nancy to attend as well. An appropriate date was chosen, and on the designated evening, we arrived at the church. Nancy saw, for the first time, the beautiful brick building that is the home of St. John Lutheran Church in Linthicum Heights, Maryland. It covers nearly an entire block in that community and is truly an impressive structure to behold.

Upon our arrival we were greeted by several members of the "call committee" and were told that the meeting was to be held at the home of the chairperson. One of the committee members volunteered to ride with us and show us the way. After about a fifteen minute drive, we reached our destination and were welcomed by the chairperson, her husband, and the remaining members of the committee. Coffee and dessert were shared, and we found the evening to be wonderfully informal and truly enjoyable as we all got better acquainted.

Much to my surprise, however, the moment arrived when the "call committee" chairperson took control of the evening. After a few preliminary remarks about the progress the committee had been making and the work they had done, she looked at me and said, "Pastor, we would like to offer you the call to be our new Senior Pastor at St. John." It was truly an unexpected development for me, and an offer I was not really prepared at that moment to accept. I was honored by their faith in my ability to lead such a large congregation and excited by the prospect, but I was also in the midst of leading another congregation – a congregation I loved – through a building program, and I owed it to them to see it through. Emotionally, I was in an immediate turmoil with all kinds of thoughts running through my head. All I could do was express my deep appreciation to them for their selection of me, tell them how honored I was to be their choice, and requested some time to think and pray before responding. They understood my position and graciously granted my request.

Driving home that evening, Nancy and I had a lot to discuss. Calvary and Woodbine had been good to us and for us, and we really hadn't thought about moving or opportunities that might exist for us down some future road. I had already declined an offer from another congregation that had expressed more than a passing interest in me becoming its next pastor and had no doubts that I had made the right decision. This, however, seemed different, and I wasn't sure what to do.

I had learned, however, to trust God's guidance – from the cross on the tree at Mar-Lu-Ridge, to how Nancy and I met, to the internship I had so enjoyed, to the importance of listening to that "still-small-voice" that speaks to us so often if we would but listen, and even to my call to Calvary. I then started to consider God's role in all that was developing for me at that time. Though I wasn't looking for a new congregation to serve, the Bishop, seemingly "out of the blue," expressed his desire to have me consider a new call and labeled me as someone who might replace him at the church he had served so faithfully and so well. And even though I considered myself less than a qualified candidate for the position, it was, much to my surprise, offered to me. None of it made much sense to me and yet there it was, and I had a decision to make. I prayed, and in my quiet times of prayer and reflection, I once again came to the realization, that God truly does place us where he wants us to be, even when we least expect it, and with that realization my decision was made. I would accept the call to St. John, but only if I could see the building project at Calvary completed!

It was August of 1984. The new church at Calvary was to be completed by late September or early October, so I requested a starting date at St. John of November 1, 1984 and my request was granted.

With sorrow and much remaining ambivalence, I submitted my resignation to the Church Council at Calvary. I know the people there loved me as I loved them, and so it was hard for all of us, and made my decision even more difficult. God then sent me another spokesman in the form of the chairman of Calvary's Building Committee. As we walked around the construction site together one day and discussed the progress being made, he stopped me for a moment to talk about my resignation. A long time farmer in the area, he was a very sincere and wonderful man, and I will never forget his words to me that day or the treasure his "down home" philosophy has been for me ever since.

Pastor," he said, "I know this is a hard time for you and for us. I know it was extremely difficult for you to make the decision you have made, and it is just as difficult for us to see you go! But, as my sister always said, 'The time to get on the train is when it is in the station.'" Obviously, he knew that there are few churches like St. John and few opportunities for pastors to be called to serve such a congregation. Even though he knew it would be hard for me to say good-bye, and the people of Calvary didn't want to lose me, he also knew that it was time for me to go and take advantage of the door God had opened for me.

I have been so grateful to that "spokesman" for that moment and always will be. He let me know, in a special way, that I was doing the right thing, and confirmed for me that it was indeed God's will that I move on.

Unfortunately, I never saw the building at Calvary completed. The inability of sub-contractors to meet their deadlines for various reasons delayed the project beyond the expected date of completion, and I left for St. John two weeks before the congregation at Calvary made its move into its new church home. I was, however, invited back to preach at the dedication, to preside at a wedding, and later to preach at the funeral of the man whose benevolence contributed so much to the project's success. Those were the only times I remember using the building, and it was everything we had all hoped it would be.

My going away party was a time for both laughter and tears. It was a time filled with many great memories of the years we had spent together, and best wishes for the future. It was a good time – a time that marked an ending and heralded a new beginning for us all.

CHAPTER 6

And He Will Raise You Up On Eagle's Wings...

According to William Barclay, a renowned New Testament scholar, "For many Christian people the Gospel according to St. John is the most precious book in the New Testament." Barclay also says when referencing the eagle, which is the emblem associated with the writer of this Gospel, that "the *eagle* stands for *John*, because the eagle of all living creatures alone can look straight into the sun and not be dazzled, and John of all the New Testament writers has the most penetrating gaze into the eternal mysteries and the eternal truths, and into the very mind of God."

I think of Barclay's words now as I reflect on what it was like for me to become the Senior Pastor of St. John Lutheran Church in Linthicum Heights, Maryland. One of the largest and most well-respected congregations in the then Maryland Synod of the Lutheran Church in America, the building itself is a large and imposing structure and the members of the church are both active and involved, and very much connected with the church's life and mission. Unlike the eagle I could not help but be dazzled by it all and, as a result, more than a little apprehensive about my ability to assume successfully the role to which God had called me.

Even the history of the church awed me. Starting as a mission in 1919, its first home was a pre-fabricated structure brought in by train and set on a foundation on Hammonds Ferry Road in Linthicum, Maryland, and its first full-time pastor was a recent seminary graduate, the Rev. Charles H. Corbett, who served the congregation from 1919-1927. In 1928, the Rev. Willis R. Brenneman became the second pastor and served until 1941.

In 1942 the Rev. Carl W. Folkemer was then called as the third pastor in the relatively new life of St. John and under his leadership, the church took off. Advised by another pastor not to accept the call since "for 23 years (St. John in Linthicum) had not grown, was still being supported financially as a 'mission congregation', and would probably never become an influence in the Lutheran Church," Dr. Folkemer obviously felt God's hand at work and, in spite of such a dire warning, moved to Linthicum.

In Dr. Folkemer's own words he summed up what occurred during his tenure by saying, *"For the next 23 years God took control of the congregation. He used an inexperienced young pastor and a small band of dedicated members and molded out of this combination a congregation that was eventually to be recognized as one of the most active congregations of the Maryland Synod."*

The metamorphosis was incredible. Under Pastor Folkemer's leadership the church thrived. It paid off its debt to the national church and grew in numbers to the extent that the pre-fabricated building, that was the church's home, was bulging at the seams. In 1944, the congregation voted to build a new and more permanent church building. A piece of property was purchased with cash and an architect hired to design a little "Village Gothic" church. Reflecting on those days Pastor Folkemer said, *"Somehow, the dreams are always the largest when one has the least money. But the dream one must have as well as the willingness to leave the 'increase' to the grace of God."*

As I heard these stories and thought about their meaning for the congregation and now for me as its new pastor, I was reminded once more in a most "dazzling" way that trusting in God's goodness and grace as we live our lives is extremely important, and that realizing how God does indeed provide for us, guide us, and speak to us is essential if we are to have a constructive relationship with Him.

With very little money in hand, the congregation still maintained its commitment to build, and so for three years, the men of the church united in a determined effort to make it happen without having to hire a contractor. What evolved, as a result, is a tremendous story of faith. Together the men gathered at the building site four evenings a week and every Saturday morning focused on achieving the extremely ambitious goal they had set for themselves. The women of the church supported the effort as well by providing coffee, meals, cakes and pies for the men as they worked.

When you think of a construction project, such as the one the members so willingly undertook, there are several essentials that come to mind. You need skilled carpenters, electricians, plumbers, and someone with the expertise to guide them all. In those days there were men within the congregation who possessed those skills – a master carpenter, a master electrician, a plumber who owned his own company and a leader with the ability to guide them and all the others who gathered to help. Eagerly and freely they donated their time and their talents and as a result, in 1951, the work was completed and the new church was dedicated.

For the next eight years the membership increased 283%; the finances increased 309%; the congregation purchased additional property for parking and for future possible development of the church building. In 1960, the people of St. John completed a large educational addition to the church as well as offices and a beautiful chapel. And, once again, in the words of Pastor Folkemer, *"The Lord was indeed in this house of believers."*

It was to this incredibly gifted and amazingly faithful fellowship of believers and dedicated disciples of Christ that I was called as the Senior Pastor, and I was indeed and, I think, understandably both "dazzled" and apprehensive. It was a large congregation. It had a history of tremendous pastoral leadership. It was comprised of people who were obviously eager to be led by and respond to God's Word. And it was a place where, as Pastor Folkemer had said, the Lord was indeed present. Being the introvert that I believe myself to be, and not always the most confident of individuals, I wondered if I was up to this particular challenge. It both excited me and concerned me. But, as I had come to realize so vividly in my life and ministry and as this congregation knew so well, the best we can do in life is to put our trust in God. My call to be the pastor at St. John was a call from God and of that I had no doubt. God must have wanted and needed me there. And with that realization I became determined to do the best I could to serve the Lord in this place with such a "dazzling" history of faith inspired works.

On November 1, 1984, I officially started my tenure at St. John. It was the beginning of twenty-five of the most wonderful and fulfilling years of my life and ministry. I learned early on that, though large in size, St. John Lutheran Church had a small church feeling. From my experience, small congregations, such as Calvary in Woodbine, Maryland, are more like families. Everyone seems to know everyone else and, as a result, the individual members and families in small churches appear to really care about one another in a special way. Large congregations, on the other hand, often come across as cold and impersonal. The greater number of members and the increased number of services on Sunday mornings, that tend to divide the membership, make it difficult for people to get to know each other well or to feel close as a body of believers. From my perspective, however, St. John was an anomaly that I celebrated. I sensed the closeness of the membership, and how each member seemed to care about the other members. They were always supportive of one another, always concerned about the needs and pains and sorrows of one another, always willing to help each other, and collectively to help those outside the church who were also hurting and in want. Again, as Pastor Folkemer had said, *"The Lord was indeed in this house of believers,"* and that was a reality I sensed throughout my years as pastor there.

Prior to my assuming the position at St. John, Pastor Folkemer had returned to serve as the interim pastor while the search for a new pastor took place. Retired by that time from his position as the Senior Pastor of Christ Lutheran Church in Baltimore, Maryland, (his home congregation), he still lived in Linthicum and so his appointment to be the interim pastor and to assist St. John in the transition that was to occur was a positive experience both for him and the congregation. In so many ways, he and the congregation had a wonderful bond that had never broken, and the mutual admiration between the former pastor and those he had once served was still strong. He had joined St. John as a member upon his retirement and would continue to be a member upon my arrival, but until then he was once again their pastor and that was good.

I didn't know him very well. His twin brother, Larry, had been one of my favorite professors in seminary, and had served, upon my request, as one of my examiners during the oral review of my thesis for the Doctor of Ministry degree. Carl Folkemer, however, I only knew by reputation, and his reputation in the Synod was outstanding. Consequently, I must admit, his presence on Sunday mornings was a bit intimidating for a young pastor like me. He was a scholar of note, a renowned preacher, and a most accomplished pastor. I hoped and prayed that I could measure up, in some small way, to what I knew he would expect from me as the senior pastor of a congregation that meant so much to him. The "self-inflicted" pressure was certainly on.

Carl, however, was a pastor in every sense of the word. He became a wonderful and trusted mentor to me, and someone who both supported and encouraged me, and who offered me wise counsel and guidance. Living only a few houses apart from one another, I would often go to see him in the evening if I had a concern or problem to work through, and we would sit in his study and discuss the issues and their resolution. He assisted me in so many ways – preaching on occasion to give me a break, covering for me when I was on vacation or deployed by the Navy, helping me with visits and home communions. St. John is a very large congregation, and I didn't have an assistant pastor. It was Carl who was always available for me, and for his help and support and love I will always be grateful.

Once more God had blessed me. Not only had He called me to serve in a wonderful congregation, but He had sent into my life someone whose wisdom and gracious counsel helped me to grow as a pastor and to understand, as I never had before, the importance of being a leader for those who had entrusted me with that role. It was also because of Carl that I had another experience with the "still small voice of God."

Approximately ten to twelve years after my arrival at St. John, Carl's health began to deteriorate. His legs grew weak and no one seemed to know why. Eventually, he underwent back surgery and returned home from the hospital a few days later. Shortly thereafter, however, he had a stroke from which he would not recover. I visited with him almost daily in the hospital, even though he was unable to respond to my presence.

Then a day arrived when I had planned to be away in order to watch my younger son play in a lacrosse game at Duke University in Durham, North Carolina. My son played for the U.S. Naval Academy, and Nancy and I did our best to make it to every one of his games. I was actually something of a "team chaplain" since, at the coach's request, I offered a prayer for the team before every game. We left on a Friday, watched the game on Saturday afternoon, and drove home shortly thereafter in order for me to be back in time for church on Sunday.

Arriving home late Saturday evening, I had the feeling that God wanted me to be with Carl. We had driven for four to five hours and it was relatively late, but I knew that I had to go to the hospital. I called Carl's wife, Margaret, told her I was going to see Carl and asked if she wanted to go with me. She responded positively, and I picked her up on the way to the hospital. We stood on each side of Carl's bed that night and shared our thoughts and feelings about the man we both loved who lay there before us. We remained like that for quite some time, listening to his labored breathing, and quietly remembering. As we held hands across the bed, I prayed, and as I spoke the "Amen" Carl sighed deeply, peacefully, and even contentedly, and then he died.

Several days later I preached at his funeral. It was one of the hardest funeral sermons I ever had to offer. But I had the feeling that God spoke through me that day, as He had spoken to me the night He told me to go to the hospital to be with Carl when he died. And through me God raised up the life of one of His most wonderful, faithful and devoted servants for all to celebrate and remember, even as He raised Carl to the new life of Easter.

I had learned a lot from Carl but, admittedly, I still had a lot to learn. The demands of a large church are vast and varied, so time management became an issue. St. John was also a church that appreciated a challenge, so having a vision and a long-range plan was also important. The larger the congregation the more visits there are to make – visits to homes and hospitals, nursing and assisted living facilities. Committee and board meetings are scheduled almost nightly, clergy meetings monthly, and more weddings, baptisms and funerals in a year than I had ever experienced. Fortunately, as a result of all the commitments I had made for myself while serving as the pastor of Calvary Lutheran Church in Woodbine, Maryland, I had learned to manage my time and to balance all the demands upon me without too much trouble. I thank God for that, and for providing the visions for St. John that ultimately came to me.

St. John is one of six congregations within the Linthicum community. The others are Episcopalian, Eastern Orthodox, Methodist, Roman Catholic, and Baptist. Unfortunately there was not a lot of collegiality among the congregations or the pastors, and nothing we tried changed that reality.

A few years into my tenure, a thought came to me to make St. John the "community church." In terms of facilities and property, we had so much to offer to the entire community and to the other congregations and that was what I wanted us to do. St. John already had a nursery school that the community used as well as meeting rooms for Alcoholics Anonymous, Al-Anon, the community quilters, a duck carving group, and various fitness and jazzercise groups, but I believed we could do more. We could do something that would involve the whole community and bring everyone together in a unique and hopefully abiding way. Once again God spoke to me, and the vision I received was of a "community fair."

Eager to pursue this new goal, I composed and sent a letter to as many community groups, churches, and organizations I could identify. I invited a representative from each to meet with me on a designated evening at St. John to discuss the development of a community fair. Only five people attended. As a result, those in attendance decided to send out one more notice announcing a new date for a similar meeting with the hope that more interested parties would attend.

At the second meeting a few more people did appear, but it was still not the response I had been anticipating. The group, however, seemed a bit more positive, and the result was that an agreement was reached to initiate a "Linthicum Community Fair." A date was chosen and a chairman was selected. I made the point, from the beginning, that this was not to be a St. John venture but a community effort. I offered the field across the street from the church as the fair's locale but emphasized that I did not want St. John tied too closely to the effort because it was important to me for all the churches to feel welcomed to participate and be involved.

The first fair was an outstanding success, and has grown phenomenally in size and structure ever since. For close to twenty years now, it has been a special event anticipated with excitement by the entire community. A parade filled with floats, political candidates, bands, cheerleaders, vintage cars and trucks, and various other participants now opens the festivities. Nearly every church in the community is represented in some way, and crafters, pony rides, bake sale tables, hamburgers, hot dogs, bar-b-que, games, silent auctions for the local PTA, and countless other offerings are available throughout the day. Entertainment – dance groups, singers, choirs – is on stage at various times throughout the fair's duration. It truly became everything I had hoped it would be, and it is one of the visions I received from God I will always treasure. Truly His Spirit was involved and was the inspiration in so many ways for an event that united a community as, perhaps, nothing else had ever done.

St. John, being the congregation it is and always has been, attracted a lot of people. As new members arrived to become part of the congregation, I would often ask what made them choose

St. John as their new church home. Invariably the response I received was that "it was such a friendly place, and a place where they felt welcomed." Growth, of course, brings with it a challenge to the available space, and even though the building that housed the St. John congregation was extremely large, it was not quite big enough. We needed new office spaces, a new space for youth ministry, a space for the music program, and additional Sunday School rooms. For the second time in my ministry, God guided me into a building program.

A committee was formed to investigate further an addition to the building. A retired engineer, with a brilliant mind and an even greater faith, served on the committee and worked closely with the contractor. Another member, who was an insurance agent with prior experience in construction, was there as well. Both of those men loved the church dearly, and their oversight of the project and concern for its successful completion was a true blessing.

As with any such project, funding was a concern. Significant contributions, however, were received from within the congregation as the work began. From that moment until the debt was liquidated, regular contributions came in steadily to the "building fund" and within approximately six years, the new building was completely paid for. It was a tremendous effort and once again, God was obviously with us to guide and inspire us in so many ways.

Again, such projects can often disrupt and even divide a congregation but not the St. John congregation. That doesn't mean that everyone was in agreement with the decision to build, but once the majority made that decision, the entire congregation seemed to give its support and joined the effort to make it happen. As the senior pastor, this is a truth I will always treasure and it exemplifies in a special way how we truly can be "one as Christ and His Father are one" if we practice the faith we profess.

During my tenure at St. John, three other major "construction" projects were undertaken and completed with the same congregational support. A new roof was put on the old building. The sanctuary, fellowship hall, and all-purpose room were air-conditioned. And in 2008, the entire sanctuary underwent a "facelift" of sorts – fresh paint, new carpet, refinished pews, new lighting, new sound system, and a remodeling of the chancel.

The latter of those three projects was unique for a special reason. As we considered what we wanted to do with the chancel and who would do the work, two of the members stepped forward. Their fathers had been very much involved with the construction of the church itself in the late 1940's and early 1950's when these two men were just small children. Having the expertise required to do the work that needed to be done in the chancel, they volunteered – as their fathers had before them – to provide the labor necessary. It was their way, I believe, to honor their fathers by following in the footsteps of the past generation and serving the church and the Lord as their fathers before them had done.

Once again I marvel at how God provides. Every day He is with us, and every day He touches us and reminds us of His presence in so many wonderful and diverse ways. Unfortunately, however, we too often fail to see the reality of this truth because we are just too busy, or just too intent on finding other, perhaps more tangible, evidence of why things happen as they do. The truth is that God certainly is active in our lives, and the sooner we acknowledge this fact the closer we will be to Him.

I have no doubt that anything I did or accomplished during my twenty-five years at St. John Lutheran Church is a result of God's guidance and inspiration. I am not a naturally creative person or an accomplished visionary, but because of that "still small voice" I learned to hear and obey, some really good things happened.

One such inspiration related to the congregation's worship life. Prior to the air-conditioning of the sanctuary, it was the practice to schedule only one service of worship on Sunday mornings throughout the summer. That service was held at 9:00 a.m. in order for the worshippers to be in an out before the sanctuary became unbearably hot – which it normally did during Maryland summers. One summer, however, I decided to offer a "campground" service of sorts outside in the church's courtyard at 8:00 a.m. It was called "Barefoot in the Courtyard" and those attending were encouraged to dress casually, pick up a folding chair to use prior to entering the courtyard, and be prepared for a brief service of word and sacrament that would last approximately thirty minutes. The order of worship was to sing a hymn (with a guitar and keyboard providing the music), read the Gospel, listen to a sermon and a prayer, celebrate Holy Communion, and close with another hymn.

The first Sunday approximately 35 people attended. By the end of the summer there were over 100, and as we prepared to resume the regular schedule in the fall no one wanted to see this new service end. As a result, we had three services every Sunday – two in the sanctuary, and one in the fellowship hall, which provided the more informal setting we had grown accustomed to in the courtyard. Over the years that service became the largest of the three. It attracted new members to the congregation and even drew in young families, since it enabled parents to worship while their children were in Sunday school. Eventually, an exceptionally talented "band" was formed to lead the music, and a paid director was added to the staff.

Not long after we had begun this particular journey, the Bishop invited the pastors of the largest congregations in the Synod to meet with a renowned church consultant who had been brought in for a day to share with us some of his thoughts about the future of the church. The first thing he did was to have all the pastors stand up. He then divided us into two groups. He asked those of us who had started something new and contemporary in terms of worship to move to one side of the room, and those who had not to move to the other. After we were so aligned, he looked at those who had not experimented with worship and said somewhat bluntly, "You are the pastors who do not want to see your churches grow!"

Not long after that experience, I realized how prophetic he was. The little summertime service I had started in the courtyard grew tremendously and became an essential part of the worship life of St. John. It was just phenomenal, and remains to this day the best attended worship service at the church. I know it was God at work once more – inspiring, guiding, directing – and providing another way for his church to grow and remain relevant for the future.

Throughout my years at St. John, God's voice and the active involvement of His Spirit guided me in so many ways, the most important being through my ministry of presence. I had learned early on that a pastor's most important role is being available to those he or she is called to serve. I, therefore, made it a point to be present for those facing surgery, those who had experienced the loss of a loved one, those who were shut-in, and those who were going through times of stress or emotional turmoil. Often this required that I be at a hospital prior to sunrise in order to meet someone who was arriving for surgery that day. Frequently, I would be there before the patient I had come to see, but this was important to me, and, as I came to realize, meant a great deal to the patient as well. While they were prepared for surgery, I would sit with their families. When the preparations were complete, I would stay with the patient, offer prayer, and not leave until the surgical team arrived to take them away. With a congregation as large as St. John, this wasn't always an easy thing to do, and at times, conflicts would arise leading me to wonder how I could be at two places at the same time. But it always seemed to work out in some strange and wonderful way, and I know that's because it was all in God's hands.

I never realized how important this part of my ministry was to the congregation until a day when I received a call from a member whose husband had suffered a serious heart attack. It was early in the morning when I got the message, and I immediately got ready and went to the hospital. When I arrived at the ward where he was being treated, a nurse looked at me and said, "He told me to expect you!" As I entered the room, he raised his head, looked at me and said, "I knew you would be here!" I spent most of the day with him and his family. His condition was serious, and he was transferred to another hospital for surgery that afternoon – surgery from which he did not recover. He was a special man, devoted to his church and faithful in so many ways, and to this day I am grateful that he had faith in me – faith that I would be with him.

Often I would receive calls from members of my church telling me of impending surgeries and usually those conversations would end with the words, "But Pastor, I don't expect you to be there. It's just too early in the morning for you to come to the hospital, so just keep me in your prayers." But they knew, as did I, that I would be there. They had come to the realization that being with them was important to me, because I knew it was important to God, who in so many ways over the years had made that clear to me.

I truly loved my ministry and my years at St. John Lutheran Church in Linthicum Heights, Maryland and the people who are that church. I was blessed in so many ways by being called there and by having those people become a part of my family. I remember the many times we laughed together, as well as the many times we cried together. And I cherish how their great faith and devotion to the church and to the Lord enriched my life, and, I pray that my ministry among them in some way enriched their lives as well.

The day eventually arrived, however, when I knew it was time to let go, and again God spoke to me. In the fall of 2008, I came down with a cold. At least I thought it was a cold! The only problem was I did not get better. When I tried to sleep on my left side at night, I had trouble breathing, and a noticeable gurgling sound was present as well. During the day I had a persistent cough and was quite congested.

After a week or so, I went to see my doctor. He prescribed an antibiotic and told me to return within a week. A week later I received another antibiotic and the same instructions. Because my symptoms failed to improve and my condition remained unchanged, I went through several different antibiotics over the course of a few weeks and a chest x-ray as well. As it turned out, I did not have pneumonia, but I was close to it.

I was also referred to an ear-nose-and throat specialist who ordered additional x-rays and scans and learned from the results that all four of my sinuses were totally infected. Even with all the antibiotics I had been taking, nothing had been powerful enough to reduce the infection. Both doctors concluded that one of the reasons this was true was that I was exhausted.

This diagnosis came as a total shock to me. I didn't feel exhausted. I never even considered what it would mean to be exhausted. Three days a week at 5:30 a.m. I worked out in a fitness center before going to church. I felt as if I had kept myself in decent shape between those work-outs and tennis and other athletic endeavors, as time permitted. My life as a Navy reserve chaplain demanded that I be prepared to pass a physical readiness test every six months, and even after I retired from the Navy, I made an effort to maintain that level of readiness. So I could not be exhausted. At least that is what I believed.

My doctors, however, felt differently, and they had my test results and their examinations to back up their conclusions. "You have to take some time off," they told me. "You have to rest!"

At first I thought that would be easy. It was early in the week when I received that news, and I decided that I could stay home for a few days, work from my office there, write my sermon, and be back in the pulpit on Sunday. But when I laid out my plan for the doctors to consider, they asked, "How many services will you celebrate on Sunday?" "Three," I responded. And the reply I got was, "Absolutely not! You need to stay home and rest for at least two weeks, or you will have an extremely difficult time beating this infection!"

So I turned over my responsibilities to my associate pastor and began a period of "forced" convalescence. I picked up some books at the bookstore Nancy and I frequented and spent my days in my study reading, meditating, praying, and reflecting on my life and ministry. And again God spoke to me.

One of the books I read was one I had heard about somewhere and just happened to spot the day we went to the bookstore. It was called *The Shack*, and as I read it I was captivated by the beauty of the story and how wonderfully it was told. I couldn't stop talking about it with Nancy, who then read it as well. It inspired me during that time I was away from church but not as one might expect.

As I considered, as a result of reading *The Shack*, how God comes to us and reveals Himself in so many different ways in order to address our needs and concerns, I began to realize, during those days at home, that God was speaking to me once more and through my body was sending me a message.

I came to the understanding that I was indeed tired – more so than I had ever imagined possible. Keeping my busy schedule,

I never allowed myself to feel exhausted, but as I sat at home I found myself sleeping more and more – basically giving my body the rest it obviously craved and demanded. As a result, I started feeling better than I had in weeks and began to consider my vision for St. John once I returned. Much to my dismay, however, I discovered that I had no vision. For over twenty years I had dreams for St. John – programs we could start, community activities we could initiate, worship services we could try, building additions and renovations we needed. I made long-range plans annually and did my best to lead the congregation forward. It was what I loved to do, especially with the people of St. John.

But sadly as I sat at home recuperating, I came to the realization that I no longer had a vision for St. John. I no longer had a goal to set for the congregation or a direction in which to lead them. And as I struggled to accept that truth, I also found myself having to accept the fact that when a pastor no longer has a vision for the congregation he has been called to serve, it is time to let go! I knew in my heart that I could stay as the senior pastor of St. John for many more years – well into my sixties, if I so desired, or even longer – such was the relationship between pastor and congregation.

I had been considering retirement, especially after turning sixty. That's only natural and is something that needs to be planned for. Still, it was just in the thinking and talking stage for the most part, and whenever I found myself standing in the sanctuary alone from time-to-time during the week, I knew it would be hard for me to leave St. John and have someone else be blessed by being called to replace me. So I didn't want to consider it too seriously, even as retirement's inevitability drew closer.

Now, however, as I sat at home, I knew it was time. It was time to accept the fact that St. John needed a new leader with a new vision, a new dream, and with the energy to move the congregation forward. It was time for me to let go!

Consequently, I made the decision with Nancy to announce my retirement at the annual meeting of the congregation in January of 2009. I had started my ministry at St. John on 1 November 1984, and would end it on 1 November 2009 – exactly twenty-five years to the day.

My last ten months in Linthicum went by quickly. I had given myself plenty of time to say good-bye, and to prepare my St. John family for the reality that, in retirement, I could not accept invitations to do weddings, baptisms or funerals. Our ties had to be severed completely in order to allow the congregation to accept a new shepherd into its midst and thus to be prepared to follow a new leader.

A few weeks before my last Sunday, I received a wonderful gift! My oldest grandson, Aiden, had not yet been baptized. He was almost five years old, and was, as he would tell everyone, my "best buddy!" Following church one Sunday morning, he asked if he could speak to me in my office. He wanted to be baptized, he told me, and his parents had agreed but wanted him to approach me about his decision and make the appropriate arrangements.

The members of the congregation had watched Aiden grow up among them and would be more than delighted to see him baptized prior to my retirement. So it was decided that I would baptize him at my very last service prior to my retirement. It was to be a very full and most memorable day!

My brother-in-law, the Rev. David Hackmann, who had preached at my service of ordination in 1973, accepted my invitation to be the liturgist that Sunday. The Rev. Dick Manning, a close friend, mentor and one of the finest preachers I have ever heard, agreed to deliver the sermon. (When Dick retired, he had requested that I preach for him, so he graciously did the same for me!) The church was packed! All of the choirs participated, and my favorite hymns and songs were played and sung. My family and special friends were all in attendance, and I experienced one of the most emotional Sunday mornings I have ever known.

My bond with the people of St. John was special, strong, and wonderful and the truth of that reality was clearly evident throughout the day. The love of a pastor for a congregation and a congregation for its pastor was clearly on display in so many ways.

The congregation had planned for my retirement for months, and the thoughtfulness, initiative, and creativity was clear. A conference/banquet hall had been reserved, guest speakers contacted, and special presentations organized. Obviously, a lot of hard work had gone into the day. I had never anticipated being so honored.

Local elected officials were on hand to present me certificates from the Maryland General Assembly, the Anne Arundel County Council, and the State Senate. Two members of the congregation had baked cakes – one depicting the stained glass windows from the church and the other depicting a book of my life and loves. High school friends and teammates were present along with a coach I had long admired. Members of the congregations I had served in Hagerstown, Maryland, and Woodbine, Maryland, were also there! In total approximately 500 people attended my retirement party, and I just couldn't believe what I was experiencing.

As each speaker concluded his or her remarks, my emotional status grew more and more shaky. This was especially true after hearing my sister speak, and then my two sons. Family had always meant so much to me, as it did to my parents, so having my sister and my sons participate that day was moving for me and so memorable.

Betty, my sister, had been a career educator. I have probably never told her how much I admired her intellect, drive, and feistiness over the years. Hopefully, now that we are both retired, I will have the chance to spend more time with her and her family and share some of those things we have never had the chance to share during our adult and professional lives.

My two sons have made me very proud. Both model very well what it is to be "tall, dark, and handsome" and both understand how hard work leads to success. Intelligent and athletic, they both always seem to have their priorities in order and live with values and morals somewhat uncommon today. They attended the same prep-school from which I graduated, and then received appointments to the U.S. Naval Academy.

Bill graduated from Annapolis in 1996 and became a surface warfare officer. Following his Second Class or junior year at the Academy, he met the daughter of one of my college fraternity brothers. They were married in 1998 and now live in Annapolis with their two sons, Aiden and Hunter. Bill spent six years on active duty in the Navy and now works for a company in

Bethesda, Maryland. His wife, Alexis, (a Morehead Scholar from the University of North Carolina) is an attorney for a law firm on Capital Hill in Washington, D.C. Bill spoke at my retirement about what it is to be a family, and I felt rewarded when he said, "My Dad always tried to be there for the people of St. John, and in spite of his hectic schedule, he was always there for us too!"

Brad, the younger of my two sons, graduated from Annapolis (where he had been an outstanding lacrosse player for four years) in 1999 and became a Naval Aviator, flying the Navy's best all-weather fighter, the F-18. He spent eleven years on active duty and had combat experience in the war on terror. He was leaving active duty at the same time I was retiring, and he had been asked to speak about my career in the Navy. In 2006, he married Missy, a lifelong member of St. John, and a graduate of Salisbury University on the eastern shore of Maryland. They live in Linthicum, Maryland, with their two children, Hailey and Blake, and still belong to St. John where Brad serves on the Congregation Council. Brad works for a company that does civilian contracting for Naval Aviation, while Missy is an elementary school Principal. Brad's words at the time of my retirement surprised me, because he knew more about my Navy career than I could have imagined. When he spoke about my experiences at the Pentagon following the tragic events of 9/11, he was visibly moved and that touched my heart as well.

Many kind things were said about me and my ministry. As the day wound down I received a new computer, was honored by having a brick purchased in my name for the new Linthicum Veterans Memorial that was being built, and Nancy and I received a retirement vacation to the Virgin Islands. The gift I will always cherish, however, is the gift of being named Pastor Emeritus of St. John. It is a gift that, for me, substantiates my twenty-five years of ministry at St. John and enables me to believe that in some small way, perhaps, how I spent my life was pleasing in God's sight.

It all began with a little cross I once found on a tree in the woods, and from that moment on I came to believe that God has been directing me and guiding me and showing me the path on which He wanted me to travel. For nearly five decades, I had done my best to heed God's call and to be God's faithful servant. Now, retired from active ministry, I humbly feel as if my life has had meaning because God has given it meaning. All I had to do was trust in Him and follow His lead, and having done my best, I can only hope that God looks upon me now, smiles, and says, "Well done, good and faithful servant!"

CHAPTER 7

God And Country

A s mentioned previously, my intention upon entering seminary to prepare for the ministry was to become a chaplain in the U.S Navy. In 1969, when I graduated from college, the United States was involved in a war in Vietnam. It was not a popular involvement by any means and one that created a great deal of controversy, anger, and discontent nation-wide. Unlike previous conflicts in the nation's history, the war in Vietnam did nothing to unite the country but created a division that was painful and one that, in many ways, changed the face of America.

In spite of the negative sentiments, I continued to find myself considering where I could best serve the Lord, and the answer was always as a military chaplain. So many of my contemporaries had been drafted into military service and were being sent to Vietnam. I thought about them often and what they were experiencing. Far away from home, walking in harm's way, they were facing trials and ordeals, fears and horrors that would no doubt have lasting effects! I wanted to minister to them. I wanted to let them know that someone cared and that God loved them. I wanted to be there for them, support them, encourage them, and share with them the good news of the Gospel.

Consequently, during my first year in seminary, I looked into what was then known as the Theological Student Program being offered by the U.S. Navy Chaplain Corps. I learned that I could be commissioned as an Ensign while I was in seminary and attend the Basic Course for chaplains during the summers between the academic years. I obtained the necessary paper work and began the process.

Prior to the completion of the application, however, I met Nancy and things changed. As we got closer and realized that we wanted to spend our lives together, she became aware of my plans and had some doubts. Not only was she being faced with the prospect of becoming a pastor's wife but also the wife of a Navy chaplain who would no doubt be going off to war. It was too much for her to process.

As a result, I held onto my application for the Navy program and focused on becoming a husband, and shortly thereafter, an ordained minister. Prior to my graduation from the seminary and my ordination in 1973, the war in Vietnam came to an end, and any guilt I was feeling about not following through on my ambition to be a minister to our troops was assuaged a bit. The desire to serve as a chaplain, however, never did!

In 1980, I took a positive step in that direction. By then I was not only a husband but also a father. My two sons, Bill and Brad, were born in 1974 and 1977 respectively. I was serving as the Senior Pastor of Calvary Lutheran Church in Woodbine, Maryland. We had bought a new house, and were enjoying our lives, our ministry, and our friends.

One of those friends was a fellow pastor and weekly golfing buddy. The Rev. Don Turley was serving as the Senior Pastor of the church where I had grown up, and where I had been both confirmed and ordained. He also had a concurrent career as a chaplain in the U.S. Army Reserve and National Guard. During our time together on the golf course, he would tell me of his duties in the Army. It was clear that what he was doing was both enjoyable and meaningful and a special part of his ministry. His words and reflections touched that part of me that still harbored a desire to serve as a chaplain, and I shared those feelings with him. In response, he promised to help me begin the process that would lead to my commission in the Army as well, and in reply I said, "If I am going to do this, I want to do it in the Navy!"

Nancy was still not enthusiastic. Even though I was envisioning a career as a reserve chaplain and not an active duty chaplain, she still realized that I could be called to active duty at any time, and that concerned her. Knowing me as she does, however, she was aware that this was important to me and putting her feelings and concerns aside, she eventually gave her blessing.

By that time I had been a parish pastor for seven years and had grown to love parish ministry. The Navy Reserve Program would give me the opportunity not only to continue that ministry path but also fulfill the destiny I had originally envisioned when I acknowledged my call to the ministry. The thought excited me, because it offered me a new challenge and a new opportunity to serve the Lord in a different way. I, therefore, requested and received permission from my congregation to begin the process that would lead to a concurrent ministerial career.

Being already ordained, the Theological Student Program was no longer an option. I needed to apply for a direct commission in the U.S. Navy Chaplain Corps, which, as I was to discover, was quite a lengthy and involved process. I had to obtain my college and seminary transcripts. I had to be endorsed as a candidate by the Lutheran Church in America, now the Evangelical Lutheran Church in America. I had to be interviewed by a senior reserve chaplain and fill out one form after another. And I had to pass a security background check, which took many months to complete.

Eventually, everything came together, and I was offered a commission as a Lieutenant Junior Grade in the U.S. Navy. I was sworn in one afternoon at an office in Hyattsville, Maryland, (just outside of Washington, D.C.) with Nancy, my two sons, and my parents as witnesses.

My first billet (or job assignment) with the Navy was as a member of the FRSA (Fleet Religious Support Activity). The unit to which I was assigned was located at the Navy Reserve Center in Baltimore, Maryland. Shortly after receiving my orders to report for duty, I was told that the entire unit was scheduled to make a trip to the Navy Base in Norfolk, Virginia, for training. Consequently, I had to purchase a uniform I didn't even know how to properly wear yet, meet with a group of chaplains I didn't know, and travel with them to a place that was like a whole new world for me, and into an existence unlike any I had ever known before. It was an unnerving experience, to say the least, and left me wondering, for a time, what I had gotten myself into.

During the time we spent in Norfolk, I never lost the feeling of being a "fish out of water." For the most part I played "follow the leader." I watched how the other chaplains boarded a ship, for example, and did my best to copy their behavior without making a fool out of myself. I wasn't sure when to salute or even how, so, I continued to watch what the others did and mimicked them time and time again. It was uncomfortable, and the uncertainty that plagued me throughout those days, and the days that followed as I worked with the unit on a monthly basis in Baltimore, was distressing.

Within a few months, however, I received orders to report to the Basic Course for Chaplains at the Navy Education and Training Center in Newport, Rhode Island. This was an eight week course designed to introduce eligible members of the clergy to life as a Navy Chaplain, and it is exactly what I desperately needed. As a reservist, I could attend the course in four week increments over a two-year period, which was best for me, since being away from the parish for two consecutive months would have been extremely difficult for me and for the congregation I was serving.

The Basic Course enabled me to experience Navy life and to learn Navy policy, procedures, and traditions. We regularly dealt with room inspections and lost privileges if the rooms failed. We marched to class, did close order drills, and were subjected to some pretty intense and demanding physical training. We learned how to wear the various uniforms correctly and stood uniform inspections as well. And, we studied and we learned. When I detached following those first four weeks and returned to the parish, I did so with a new found confidence in my decision to affiliate with the Chaplain Corps, and an eagerness to return to Newport to complete my training and get on with my Navy career.

Over the course of the following twenty-six years, that career enriched my life and my ministry in so many ways. It opened doors and opportunities for me that enabled me to have experiences, create new relationships, and see things that I will both treasure and ponder for the rest of my life.

Navy chaplains are assigned to provide ministry not only for Navy personnel but also for those who are serving in the Marine Corps and with the Coast Guard. Not often does a chaplain have an opportunity to serve all three throughout the course of his or her career, especially as a reservist, but fortunately I was an exception. Over the years I received orders to serve with the Navy, Marine Ground and Air units, and eventually with the Coast Guard as well. Each assignment was special for me, and I developed a great and lasting appreciation for all the young men and women of those various organizations who willingly volunteer to serve our great nation as members of the armed forces.

One extremely unique assignment for me, however, enabled me to serve for a time with my older son, Bill. The destroyer he was assigned to was returning to its homeport in Portsmouth, Virginia, following a lengthy deployment. The chaplain on board was leaving the ship in Puerto Rico and a request had apparently been made to have another chaplain join the ship for the remainder of the voyage home. I requested and received the orders to be the replacement chaplain.

The ship arrived in Puerto Rico at night, and I was on the pier to witness its approach. It was raining, so I was invited to wait in a truck parked nearby until the ship was ready to receive visitors. When it was appropriate, I approached the gangplank and was piped aboard. I was met on the quarterdeck by a young petty officer who had been sent to escort me to the ship's administration office. On the way he asked, "Sir, are you related by any chance to Lieutenant Gilroy?" In reply, I proudly stated, "Lieutenant Gilroy is my son!"

Bill was serving as the ship's Assistant Administration Officer. We shared the same quarters for the remainder of the cruise, ate together in the officer's mess, and even spent time on the bridge together at night when I went there to offer the evening prayer, and he was serving as the Officer of the Deck. It was a proud moment for me and one of my most memorable experiences in the Navy.

In so many ways, in spite of Nancy's initial reluctance, we became a Navy family. Bill had decided, while in junior high school that he wanted to attend the Naval Academy, and on induction day I gave him the oath of office. Three years later Brad followed his brother to Annapolis, and I swore him in as well. When Brad finished flight school and received his wings, I flew to Texas to pin those wings on his chest. When Bill was selected for promotion, I once again led him through the oath. When Brad deployed for the first time, I was there to see him fly off to his ship, and when he graduated from the Navy's famed Fighter Weapons School, or Top Gun, I was there for the ceremony. Nancy, of course, was always present as well, and regardless of her misgivings about any of us having Navy careers, she was a proud and exceptional Navy wife and mother. Together we shared a lot as a result of the Navy, and we all have memories we will cherish forever, and for those memories and those experiences I am most grateful.

During the course of my career, I was selected to be a Commanding Officer three times – once with a Navy unit, once with a Marine unit, and once with the Coast Guard. The Coast Guard command billet was a national command billet, which means that I was responsible for all the Navy reserve chaplains nationwide who were assigned to the U.S. Coast Guard. It was probably my most exciting, fulfilling, and meaningful command. I worked directly with the Chaplain of the Coast Guard at Coast Guard Headquarters in Washington, D.C., and developed the position of Deputy Chaplain of the Coast Guard for Reserve Affairs. It was during my time at Coast Guard Headquarters that I was involved in what was probably the most intense, traumatic, and emotional ministry of my life, and one of the most unforgettable and infamous moments in our nation's history.

On 11 September 2001, I was in my office at the church when our bookkeeper came in to tell me his wife had called to let him know that a plane had just flown into the World Trade Center in New York City. Wheeling a television into the office, we gathered with the church secretary and others who were in the building at the time to watch the events that were unfolding. As we watched, the second plane hit the second tower and reports came in about the plane that had hit the Pentagon and the one that had gone down in a field in Pennsylvania. Shocked and dismayed by what we had seen we realized, as did the entire country, that life as we had known it was suddenly changing before our very eyes.

Later that afternoon, I was called to active duty and told to report the following morning to the Office of the Chief of Navy Chaplains in Washington, D.C.. That office was located in the Navy Annex, which is on a hill overlooking the Pentagon. I had been there many times before in my Navy career, but never under such difficult circumstances, and never with the expectation of seeing the things I was about to see upon my arrival on 12 September 2001.

At 0700 (7:00 a.m.) on the day after the terrorist attack, the Pentagon was still smoldering. The plane that had attacked the Pentagon had passed directly over the Navy Annex the day before. The active duty chaplains, who had witnessed the attack, stood with me that morning and told me that as the plane passed over, the pilot gave full thrust to its engines as he clipped the light poles on the Pentagon parking lot and dove into the building.

My duties in Washington were many and varied. My first day there I was a part of a CACO team. CACO stands for Casualty Assistance Calls Officer. It is a team of officers, including a chaplain, who have the task of visiting with the families of those who are missing in a tragedy such as the one that had just occurred. It is not an easy task. The next day I spent in the Navy Annex working on duty rosters and counseling. Those who had either survived or witnessed the attack had much to share and desperately needed to talk. The third day I worked at the site of the attack. A chapel tent had been erected there, and this gave us a place to hold worship services and counsel as well. During my time there, I also worked with the mortuary team – the team tasked with the recovery and proper disposition of those who had perished in the attack. My fourth day I spent at the Family Assistance Center, which had been set up in a hotel in Crystal City, not far from the Pentagon. It was there that the families of those who were missing could come to receive reports about the progress being made at the site. As anyone might imagine, it was an extremely emotional place to be. On the Sunday following the attack, I was chosen to accompany those families as they were taken by bus to a hillside overlooking the Pentagon. It was there that they could see, for the first time, the extent of the damage caused by the attack, and for many of them it offered an opportunity for closure as they began to accept the fact that many who were missing would probably not be found. For the days that followed, I continued to rotate through those various duty stations until my time came to an end and I returned home.

I will never forget what I saw there, what I did there, and what I felt there. How anyone can be so evil as to inspire others to give their lives and in that self-sacrifice destroy the lives of so many innocent people is beyond my ability to comprehend. And yet as I stood in the rubble of that evil deed, I found myself overcome time and time again by the goodness and love that surrounded me there as well, and felt as I never had before the presence of God in a most powerful way.

Upon my return to my ministry at St. John Lutheran Church in Linthicum Heights, Maryland I wrote a message for our monthly newsletter and shared my thoughts about my experiences at the Pentagon with my congregation. In that writing I sought to share my feelings with the people I loved and served as a pastor, and hoped that through my words they might be comforted by the knowledge that God is indeed with us in good times as well as bad and that if we just open our hearts and our eyes, we will be able to see and hear Him. With that in mind, this is what I wrote:

Yesterday afternoon I finished a tour of active duty as a Navy chaplain in Washington, D.C.. I was called late in the day on September 11th to report the following morning to the Navy Annex overlooking the Pentagon. Chaplains were needed to minister to the rescue workers and the families of those victimized by an unconscionable act of terror and violence.

I know a part of me will always be there at that site. Those of us who shared the experience will never forget what we saw there, or what we did there. Like the rest of the country, we will never be the same again as a result of what took place on September 11th. Indeed, the entire world has been changed by what happened that day, and only time will tell what lies before us in the weeks, months, and years to come.

Still, in the midst of life's uncertainties, I do know one thing for sure. I know God is with us. I saw Him at the Pentagon. Through the flames and the smoke, the exhausted and tormented looks on the faces of the rescue workers, and the watchful eyes of those who stood guard with weapons at the ready, God came to us who were there, and delivered to us His hope and His peace.

God revealed Himself in the Baptist Men's Group from North Carolina who drove to Washington, D.C., in a huge truck and set up a place on the parking lot where they could prepare meals for the rest of us. From beef stroganoff, to chicken and dumplings, they cooked for and handed out hot meals to all who came by to see them, and did so with a smile and a word of thanks for the sacrifices that others were making.

God revealed Himself to us in the Red Cross worker who walked among us handing out thank you notes from people throughout the country, as well as blankets for when the nights grew cold, ponchos when the rains came, and anything else we might need throughout the days and nights we were there.

God revealed Himself in the Salvation Army workers who also gave out hot meals and supplies, as well as Bibles and encouragement.

God revealed Himself in the McDonalds and Burger King people who drove in with trailers that converted into restaurants and gave out burgers, fries, chicken and drinks free of charge.

God revealed Himself in the civilians who clustered on the hill above the Pentagon each night for a candlelight vigil, and to leave flowers, flags, prayers, and scripture verses as adornments for the fence surrounding Arlington Cemetery.

God revealed Himself in the experienced FBI agent who came to me one day and said, "Chaplain, I can't leave the site to which I have been assigned, so do you think you could arrange for us to have a Mass here on Sunday?" I asked if he could get me a tent, and before the day was over, that tent was set up, and a chapel established at his site. On the following Sunday there was both a Protestant service and a Catholic mass offered for those who continued to work there, as well as daily devotions, and a place where those who were troubled by what they had seen could come and talk.

God revealed Himself in the infantry General who was tasked with the responsibilities of the Family Assistance Center. It was there that the families of those who were missing could come for briefings twice a day with the hope that the information they hungered for would be available to them. His was a most difficult duty, but every morning he gathered his chaplains around him for a prayer, and every morning his prayers were better than those of us who were the chaplains. He was obviously a man of great faith whose faith influenced his life. He needed to pray. He needed to feel God with him, since he felt so deeply for those who gathered before him to learn of those they loved. And God was indeed with him.

God was there in so many ways. He shared in our grief. He lifted us in our moments of despair. He gave us strength. He enabled us to look beyond the present and to focus once more on the promised future made possible for all people of faith by His Son, Jesus. He helped us to see in the midst of such a horrible tragedy how much better the world would be if we would just love each other as He loves us, not just when tragedy strikes, but always.

We needed God's visible presence at such a time, and God did provide that presence for us. He is always near to us if we just keep our eyes open. Hopefully, we will learn from this experience our need to always be near to Him....

In 2006, I retired from the Chaplain Corps of the United States Navy at a ceremony held at St. John. I had just completed a tour as the Chaplain for the Commander of the Submarine Force Atlantic and had worked in the Office of Operational Ministries for the Atlantic Fleet. Having attained the rank of Captain and nearing the age of sixty, my career was obviously drawing to a close, so I submitted my retirement papers. I did not really want a formal ceremony to mark that occasion, but the Navy insisted. I only consented after those in charge agreed to my request that the ceremony be held in the church I was serving, so that the congregation that had supported my military ministry in so many ways could share in the occasion.

My Navy career had enriched my life with many memorable experiences. I had been given the opportunity to write two historical monographs relative to the Chaplain Corps of the U.S. Navy that were published and distributed to every active duty and reserve chaplain. I had slept in the mud and navigated through swamps in the dead of night with the Marines. I had offered evening prayer for the crew of a destroyer at sea. I had socialized with Marine aviators (fighter pilots) in Key West, Florida, and led chapel services at the Naval Air Station in Bermuda. I had counseled recruits struggling with the demands of Coast Guard boot camp in Cape May, New Jersey, and plebes overwhelmed by the stresses of plebe summer at the Naval Academy. I had patrolled along the coast off Ocean City, Maryland, on a Coast Guard Cutter. And, as a result of the events of 9/11, I had a taste of what it means to minister to those afflicted by acts of terrorism.

All along the way, God's hand was there to guide me, and in many, many ways God made His presence known to me and to those I served and served with. I will forever be appreciative of the fact that God called me to this unique, special, and wonderful ministry and by so doing, enabled me to touch even more lives in His name. My military ministry was rich and full in so many ways; and I thank God for providing me with the opportunity to serve as a chaplain.

CHAPTER 8

The Priesthood Of All Believers

The Priesthood of All Believers is a doctrine I have always treasured and taken very seriously and is one that was actually personified for me on the day of my ordination in a very vivid way. As was customary, all of the ordained clergy attending that ceremony were vested, and some were participating. However, a friend of mine, who was also participating as a lector. was not ordained but was a young man who had once seriously considered entering the ministry.

At the point in the service when the candidate is actually called forth to be ordained by the Bishop, the members of the clergy, who are present, are also invited to come forward to join the Bishop in the laying on of hands. The candidate kneels before the Bishop, the attending clergy surround him or her, and the Bishop and the clergy place their hands on the candidate's head as he or she is ordained as "a Minister of the Church of Christ in the Office of

Word and Sacraments according to the Confession and Order of (the then) Lutheran Church in America."

Prior to my service of ordination, I found myself standing next to the Bishop as we awaited the beginning of the procession into the church. I spoke to him of my friend and inquired as to whether it would be appropriate, since he was participating in the service, to have him come forward and join in the laying on of hands.

Without a moment's hesitation, the Bishop looked at me and said, "Bill, I know you understand the meaning of the priesthood of all believers, so it would certainly be most appropriate for him to join us!"

To this day there is one picture from my ordination service I cherish for its extremely special meaning. The only thing you see in the picture is a group of clergy in their robes and stoles holding out their hands to me, and there in their midst – distinguished among them by his lack of vestments – is my friend whose hand is also extended along with theirs.

That picture will forever stand for me as a truly unique depiction of what "the priesthood of all believers" is about, and it is something I always refer to whenever I attempt to explain that doctrine to others. The clergy in the picture obviously have a special calling – a calling to the ministry of Word and Sacraments. That calling, however, doesn't make them **more** special individually, since, as Luther says, "...*there is no, true, basic difference between laymen and priests (pastors), princes and bishops, between religious and secular, except for the sake of office and work, but not for the sake of status. They are all of the spiritual estate.... But they do not all have the same work to do. Every believer has priestly authority by virtue of his baptism.*"

By virtue of our baptisms, we are essentially the same. We are men and women loved and cherished by God and called to be God's own and to do God's will, which is to love, forgive, and care for one another as brothers and sisters in Christ.

Throughout my ministry, I have striven to emphasize that teaching and to encourage the congregations I have served to understand that ministry is a joint endeavor. It is a pastor and congregation working in harmony to care for one another, to rejoice in God's love, and to proclaim that love through words and deeds within the community of believers and throughout the community existing beyond the walls of the church. It is all of the baptized understanding God's call to be like pastors to one another and to those outside their circle of believers.

I never wanted to be placed on a pedestal as a result of the collar I wore or the stole around my neck. I never wanted to be considered "better" than those I served, because I am not. I wanted my congregations to know that I would always be there for them, and that they should always be there for each other and for the world around them as well, and that ministry is something to which God calls us all in one way or another.

As St. Paul once said, *"Now there are varieties of gifts, but the same Spirit; and there are varieties of services, but the same Lord; and there are varieties of activities, but it is the same God who activates all of them in everyone. To each is given the manifestation of the Spirit for the common good."* (I Corinthians 12:4-7 NRSV)

In other words, we all have gifts to share – gifts with which God has blessed us – and God calls us to use the gifts with which we have been blessed for one purpose, "the common good."

Or, as St. Paul goes on to say, *"For just as the body has many members, and all the members of the body, though many, are one body, so it is with Christ. For in the one Spirit we were all baptized into one body... and we were all made to drink of one Spirit.... Now you are the body of Christ and individually members of it. And God has appointed in the church first apostles, second prophets, third teachers; then deeds of power, then gifts of healing, forms of assistance, forms of leadership, various kinds of tongues."* (I Corinthians 12:12-13, 27-28 NRSV)

And again it is emphasized that though we are as different as the various parts of the human body are different, we are each important to the body if the body is to remain healthy. We are each called upon to use the talent that is ours for the good of all, so that the body remains strong and vital rather than weak and handicapped.

This is why I believe the priesthood of all believers to be so important. It doesn't set any one of us apart from the others but emphasizes that we are all like priests or pastors. God needs each and every one of us working together if His Kingdom is to grow and be fruitful, and if we ever hope to be pleasing in His sight.

Fortunately, my various calls to the congregations I served enabled me to see this doctrine adhered to in all of its glory, and to experience first-hand its importance and meaningful expression.

So often on a Sunday morning when the announcements were being made prior to worship, I found myself having to inform the congregation that someone had just joined "the Church Triumphant" or that someone was seriously ill. Most of the time that news came as a shock to the majority of the members who were present that day, and as the words left my mouth, an audible gasp of surprise and concern could be heard from those who were gathered. It was gratifying for me as the pastor to realize just how much the members of that congregation really cared about each other. It was even more gratifying when, throughout the days that followed, calls would come from members who desired to inquire as to what could be done to help the family that was struggling. Someone they loved was hurting, and they wanted to help. Someone they loved was dealing with a crisis, and they wanted to offer themselves as care givers in whatever way they could.

In so many ways, the members of the congregations I served understood and embodied Luther's belief in the priesthood of all believers. They took seriously their call to care for others in need and to be like pastors to one another, and it was a beautiful thing to see and experience and something I constantly rejoiced in throughout my ministry.

Eventually, as a result of their understanding of their own call to ministry, the members of St. John Lutheran Church in Linthicum, Maryland, associated with the Stephen Ministry program and trained leaders who then trained those who had volunteered to be Stephen Ministers. Their commitment to that unique and special one-on-one ministry was fantastic, and the work they did was so meaningful. As care givers, the Stephen Ministers at St. John embraced in so many ways the care receivers to whom they were assigned, and time and time again I would hear from those care receivers just how much their Stephen Minister meant to them. The Stephen Ministers assisted their care receivers as the care receiver dealt with the loss of a loved one, or struggled with a disease that was debilitating or even life-threatening, or felt lonely, or just needed someone to talk to. They cared deeply for the person to whom they ministered, and that care or love was evident and enriched the lives of both the care giver and the care receiver.

Truly the people I served understood what the priesthood of all believers meant and took it to heart. As a result, many were blessed by the ministry provided, and that includes me.

There are times, after all, when the pastor needs a pastor. Theoretically, the role of the Synod Bishop in the Evangelical Lutheran Church in America is to be the "pastor to the pastors." In practice I never experienced the validity of that definition except for the Bishop who ordained me. He was there to offer wise counsel from time to time and that was appreciated. For the most part, the Bishops I knew and worked with were focused more on the administrative duties the office demanded. Perhaps this was out of necessity! From my perspective, however, it was basically a political position, and the person in that position had to deal with aspects relative to the church that were not appealing to me – from congregations in conflict, to pastors in trouble, to statements and policies being issued by the church at large that challenged our theology and understanding of scripture. It was not a position to which I aspired or one that I ever fully appreciated.

As a result, whenever I found myself in need of pastoral care, I seldom approached the Bishop. Fortunately, I had a tremendous support group comprised of three very special pastors, who became in so many ways my mentors and close friends. Three men I knew would always be there for me, if I needed anything. Since I care for them so much and treasure their friendship and love I would be remiss if I did not mention their names – the Rev. Donald Turley, the Rev. Richard Manning, and the Rev. Dr. Carl Folkemer. These men were exceptional pastors and leaders - respected and admired by all who knew them. I owe them a lot and will never forget what they did to guide and support me through the years.

However, I also had another source for personal pastoral care, which once again reflects the validity of the priesthood of all believers. That source was the people who called me to be their pastor. Through them God made his presence and love known to me in so many ways. And when circumstances in my life and the lives of my immediate family members dictated a need for pastoral care, they provided that care in an exceptional way and, by so doing, brought the hope that God promises to us all.

In 1974, while Nancy was expecting our first child, her mother, who was only forty-seven years old at the time, suffered a stroke. Nancy's parents lived on the eastern shore of Maryland, in a little town called Princess Anne, which was about a 3.5 to 4 hour drive from St. Mark's Lutheran Church in Hagerstown, Maryland, where I was serving as an assistant pastor. We had taken a few days off to spend some time in Princess Anne with her family prior to our child's birth, and so we were there when her mother was taken ill. I sincerely believe God directed us to choose that time for our visit, so Nancy could have a few good hours with her mother prior to the stroke's arrival, and for that we were thankful.

For several days, Nancy's mother was in intensive care, but the signs were not good. The stress put Nancy into a false labor, and she was also hospitalized briefly as a result. Unfortunately, Nancy's mother never regained consciousness and passed away.

I had notified the Senior Pastor with whom I was working at the time, and he informed the congregation. We had only been there for a little over a year by then, but we had been well received and had made some good friends.

To our surprise and great joy, one of those families, the Grays, arrived in Princess Anne within hours after I had notified the church. They drove a significant distance to be with us, and their presence and love lifted our spirits as they comforted us and embraced us and offered us pastoral care. They were and always have been a gift from God for our family.

Several years later, in 1983, our younger son, Brad, was taken ill. Once again, we were spending a few days on the eastern shore of Maryland, and he went into respiratory distress. We rushed him to a local hospital, and his condition continued to deteriorate. That hospital contacted the renowned Johns Hopkins Hospital in Baltimore, Maryland, to seek advice relative to his condition. It was decided that he had to be airlifted to Hopkins as quickly as possible.

When the helicopter arrived to transport Brad, one of the doctors decided he would fly along to continue to care for Brad. Another doctor told us, as the helicopter lifted off for the flight, that chances were Brad would not survive the trip.

With that on our minds we set out on the two-hour drive to Baltimore. Upon our arrival we were taken to the Pediatric Intensive Care Unit at Hopkins where a doctor met us to gather information about Brad. He told us he believed he knew what was happening, but it was so rare he had to be sure. As it turned out, God was once again present. That doctor had studied under the doctor who had discovered an infection known as "toxic shock syndrome." It was more common in females, however, and not something normally seen in a five-year old boy. Brad, however, was the exception.

He spent a week in intensive care, and we never left his side. During that week the members of the church I was serving at the time, Calvary Lutheran Church in Woodbine, Maryland, rallied around us. Every night another family came to the hospital to bring us dinner. They also brought us a poster that was to be hung on the wall at the foot of Brad's bed. The poster was a prayer circle. The congregation had arranged for a member to be at the church every hour on the hour to pray for Brad's recovery. The circle showed each hour of the day for that week, and the name of the person who would be praying at that time. The poster became a very special part of Brad's recovery. The nurses were amazed by what was taking place at Calvary, and they would check the chart and ask us about the person who was praying during a particular time.

Brad spent two weeks at Hopkins, and conquered the infection that had so threatened him. When he returned home, his Sunday school teacher, a wonderful, young woman named Nancy Stockdale, arrived at our house one evening dressed as a clown. She brought with her a box of presents for Brad. The presents had been gathered by the congregation as a welcome home gift. There were over thirty wrapped packages in that box, which truly thrilled a little boy's heart. And just so his brother, who was older by three years, didn't feel left out, there was also a box of presents for him. They had thought of everything, and they were God's gift to us all. The ministry they provided for us was wonderful, and it is something we will never forget.

Brad grew to be 6'4" and 220 lbs, and was an outstanding high school and college athlete. After graduating from the U.S. Naval Academy, he flew F-18 Hornets, the Navy's most sophisticated all-weather fighter plane, and was involved in the war on terrorism. He is married now and has two children of his own. We thank God every day for him!

Then in 1999, while in surgery, my mother passed away. She had been a cancer survivor for close to thirty years, but as a result of her cancer, her bones had become brittle as she aged and one night, while turning over in bed, she broke her hip.

I sat with her prior to her surgery, and we prayed together. During surgery, however, a blood clot formed and went to her heart. She did not survive.

My parents had joined St. John Lutheran Church in Linthicum, Maryland, where I had been the Senior Pastor since 1984. They loved the congregation and were loved in return. They had made many friends and enjoyed the fellowship to be found there.

At my request Pastor Don Turley officiated at the service held in the sanctuary. He came back from his vacation just to be there for us, and I appreciated his willingness to do so. At that moment, I just wanted to be a part of the family. I knew that, though I was her pastor as well as her son, I could not fulfill that role for her that day.

Don's words and remembrances were comforting, as was the congregation's support. The church can seat about 400 people, and there had to be at least that many people there. They surrounded us with love, offered us the comfort of their presence, thoughtfulness and kindness, and embraced us at a time when we needed to be so held. God was with them, and through them He was especially with us.

A year and a half later, Dad joined Mom. He never fully recovered from her loss and deteriorated quickly in her absence. He knew that he would be with her again when he died and shared that feeling with those who were close to him. He had such great faith, and I knew he would be happy when he realized the reunion with her in heaven he so longed for.

Again the members of St. John Lutheran Church were there for us. The memorial service was packed. Even Navy Chaplains I was serving with, at the time, attended from their offices in Washington, D.C., and one of them requested the opportunity to speak. At that time he was the Chaplain of the Coast Guard, and I was the Deputy Chaplain of the Coast Guard for Reserve Affairs. An outstanding preacher, he didn't know Dad, but his comments touched me deeply and so impressed those who were there that day. God was surely with him, and as a result, God touched all of us through his words.

Over the years Nancy and I found ourselves hospitalized for various reasons. Each time the members of the congregations we were serving reached out to us, cared for us, **ministered** to us. They became our pastors and filled that role extremely well.

God blessed us in so many ways throughout the course of my ministry by providing care for us through the presence of others – clergy and lay alike – who took seriously their own call to ministry and their efforts to heed that call were a blessing to me and to my entire family. In them I saw and felt God, time and time again, as through them God's love and constant presence was personified, and in them the doctrine of "the priesthood of all believers" was fulfilled.

God's Amazing Grace

The word **grace** is defined as "unmerited divine assistance given man for his regeneration or sanctification." It is also considered to be "a virtue coming from God," or, to put it another way, "a gift from God."

Throughout my life and ministry, I have come to experience, understand, and appreciate God's grace in a myriad of ways. The most important, of course, is the gracious gift of God's Son, our Lord and Savior Jesus Christ, and the forgiveness, hope, and life that gift of grace makes possible for all those who believe in Him. There are, however, other less significant ways, perhaps, in the greater scheme of things, where I have realized God's amazing grace and have had my life both touched and enriched as a result.

As mentioned in previous chapters, like all young men and women, I had visions and dreams relative to what I wanted to do with my life, and like all your men and women, those visions and dreams frequently changed as I matured and my horizons expanded.

Encouraged strongly by my grandfather, I had once considered following in his footsteps, becoming a mortician, and eventually taking over and carrying on, for another generation, the business he so loved and which so defined his life. That was a fleeting vision at best, and though I knew I would be disappointing him, I began to move away from what was really his vision for me more than my own.

I entered college with the hope of becoming a teacher and coach, so that I could return to the school in Baltimore from which I had graduated, and which I loved, and continue my relationships there for years to come. That vision also faded, however, as I began to appreciate the other opportunities my college education would afford me professionally.

As a result, pre-law became my focus. The summer after my freshman year, I met with an attorney, who was an old friend of my families, and discussed with him the various aspects of a legal career. The opportunities excited me, and I continued my studies in the fall with law school as my new goal.

At the same time, the war in Vietnam seemed to be escalating and more and more troops were being committed to Southeast Asia. College graduates were not exempt from serving, so I also had to consider how that would affect my graduation plans. The Marine Corps Officer Candidate Program became a possibility for me and one I had to consider as well as my application to law school.

During my junior year of college, however, God really took over, and my call to the ordained ministry, of the then Lutheran Church in America, inspired my personal career path from that moment on. In retrospect I now realize and fully understand that the ministry was truly the path I was destined to take. It is where God wanted me to be, and what He wanted me to do with my life. It was what the talents with which He had blessed me were meant for, and truly as I look back on my life and ministry, I do so with the confidence that God knew what was best for me and guided me where He wanted me and needed me to be throughout the course of my career. My visions and dreams, though far from frivolous, were not exactly the kinds of careers for which I was best suited, and God, who always knows what is best for us, helped me to understand that truth and led me down the path that was best for me.

It was a career path full of meaningful and memorable rewards – not in a material sense, but in ways so much more important and valuable. And yet, as if those rewards were not enough God, by his wondrous grace, also found ways to reward me by presenting me with incredible opportunities along the way that allowed me to experience, as well, the fulfillment of some of my original and personal life dreams.

I returned to Boys' Latin, my old prep school, as something of a part-time chaplain. I began as a member of the Alumni Board. I was then invited to give the invocation and benediction for the opening convocation of school in the fall, the closing convocation in the spring, and the commencement exercises for the graduating seniors. I also prayed at ground breakings, building dedications, and homecoming luncheons and reunions. I officiated at memorial services, and once was invited to give the commencement address, which was a special honor for me, and one I will always remember. I served on the Board of Trustees for eight years and chaired several of the Board's committees. Both of my sons followed me to Boys' Latin, and I prayed at their respective graduation ceremonies. I continued my relationship as the "unofficial school chaplain" for well over thirty years, and eventually decided it was time to retire the year I also retired from my congregational ministry.

My vision of one day becoming a coach was also realized, as again, God gave me some truly special opportunities at so many different levels. In college I joined several of my fraternity brothers as employees of the Hickory, North Carolina, Bureau of Recreation. We were hired to coach the elementary school basketball teams in Hickory and to officiate at the games being played in the PTA Volleyball League. I had one team of boys and one team of girls, and my girls team won the city championship my senior year.

After enrolling as a student at the Lutheran Theological Seminary in Gettysburg, Pennsylvania, I was informed that Gettysburg College was looking for an Assistant Lacrosse Coach for its relatively new lacrosse program. I interviewed for the position, was hired, and served as the team's assistant coach for two years. Being just a year or two older than the players, I often suited up and scrimmaged with them in order to demonstrate what I wanted them to do. Often, as a result of the practice and game schedule, I would miss dinner at the seminary, but the players would invite me to join them at their respective fraternity houses on those nights, and I ate with them.

While serving at St. Mark's in Hagerstown, I got involved with the lacrosse program at a private school in the area. I joined the coach there in forming a club lacrosse team for adults to compete in the Central Atlantic Lacrosse League. We both played for that team, became friends, and I assisted him, unofficially, from time to time with his team.

Later I coached my two sons through their recreation lacrosse years and watched them play for the same preparatory school where I had learned to love the game. The recreation teams they played for and which I coached produced some incredible talent. Many of those players went on to play in what is considered to be the best high school league in the country, and subsequently, at the collegiate level.

My desire to become a chaplain in the U.S. Navy upon my graduation from seminary and ordination, which I decided to abandon after asking Nancy to marry me, was also eventually fulfilled when God, through a good friend, opened that door for me as well.

Becoming a chaplain in the U.S. Navy Reserve was something I never regretted doing and provided me with two exceptionally fulfilling and meaningful careers in ministry.

God so graciously loves and cares for us that He never forgets. He never forgets what it is that can make us happy and fulfilled. He never forgets what it takes to make our dreams come true. And somehow He finds a way to reach out to us and guide us, if we would but follow Him down pathways through life that lead to often unimaginable joys and life enriching experiences.

He does this in so many wonderful ways – through an unexpected message delivered by a friend, through an unexpected opportunity that is suddenly offered, through the wise counsel of a treasured mentor, or the encouragement of a loved one. He finds so many ways to reach out to us and through us, not just to let us know His will for us, but also to enable us to fulfill our own envisioned destinies successfully, even as we do His will. I know this to be true. I remember the many ways He has used others to make His will for me known, the many experiences through which He has touched and guided my life, and the many wondrous ways in which His "still small voice" has spoken to me.

I also believe God has even worked through me to touch the lives of others. While attending the U.S. Navy Chaplain School, which was then located in Newport, Rhode Island, I had planned to visit my sister and her husband in New York one weekend. I was unable to do so because all of the rooms my class was using in the barracks failed weekly inspection, and we were all required to stand for that inspection again on a Saturday morning. Since I could not leave Newport, I invited my sister and her husband to visit me. They accepted, since they had never been to Newport, and as a result, a dream for them came true.

They both loved New England, but there were very few Lutheran churches in New England to which Dave, my brother-in-law, could be called. One of those churches, however, was in Newport, and the chaplain who was the Basic Course Officer (the officer in charge of the Basic Course for Chaplains I was attending) was serving as that congregation's interim pastor. Knowing all of this, I spoke with him about Dave and his interest in pursuing a call to the New England Synod of the then Lutheran Church in America, and he arranged a meeting for Dave with that church's Call Committee (the search committee tasked with the responsibility of finding the congregation a new pastor). Dave, who really had not come prepared in terms of appropriate attire for such an occasion, met with the committee and appropriately impressed them. He was subsequently called to be their pastor and remained there until his retirement from the ministry twenty-five years later.

Our rooms had never failed an inspection until that weekend. We were all convinced it was a planned failure so that we might experience the disappointment known by enlisted personnel when "leaves" (weekend passes allowing for absence from base) are cancelled. Yet, as a result, something good happened for someone I cared for. A new opportunity arose for Dave, one I believe he really prayed for, and one which brought both him and my sister the fulfillment of a dream. Following their respective retirements, they remained in their beloved New England and presently live happily in the home they designed and had built on a beautiful lake in New Hampshire.

Truly God was again at work here providing unexpected opportunities through unique circumstances and by so doing to touch and meaningfully change someone's life.

I also believe I was the conduit through which He called others to the ordained ministry of His church. While I was serving as the Senior Pastor of St. John Lutheran in Linthicum, Maryland, four young members of the congregation heard and accepted God's call to serve Him as a pastor. In all humility I can't and won't accept the credit for this. They were all very special young people, who were extremely active throughout their lives within a congregation that loved and nurtured them as they grew in their faith. The Spirit was already within them in so many ways, and all they needed was a word of encouragement to listen to what God was saying to them. All I did was what one of my former pastors once did for me. I just told them, from time to time, that they should consider going to the seminary. As a result, St. John gained the reputation, which was once verbally expressed by one of the Bishop's assistants, as an "anomaly among the Synod's congregations," since so many of our young members were going into the ministry. This was something I have always been proud of and speaks volumes about what St. John Lutheran Church in Linthicum, Maryland, was about.

Today one of those young people is close to finishing seminary, and three are serving as pastors within various congregations – two as Senior Pastors and one as an Assistant Pastor on the staff of a very large congregation. I continue to hear from them and know that they are all doing well.

In a uniquely wonderful way, God also enabled me, or used me as an instrument, to provide life-enriching and fulfilling experiences for both of my sons. As a parent, of course, I sincerely hope I have always played a significant role in some way in their lives.

But there came a time when an opportunity arose unexpectedly and as a result, they were each introduced to the young women who would become their wives.

On the twenty-fifth anniversary of my graduation from Lenoir Rhyne College (now University), I decided to attend the school's homecoming event and reconnect with classmates and fraternity brothers who would also be there for the class reunion. It was the first time I had ever returned for a homecoming weekend.

One of my fraternity brothers, who was also in my graduating class, was there with his wife and their two youngest children. We had not seen each other since our graduation day twenty-five years earlier. Sitting together at the football game, I showed him pictures of my two sons. My younger son was in high school at the time and did not make the trip with us. My older son was in his Second Class (or Junior) year at the Naval Academy. Upon seeing Bill's picture, in which he was wearing his parade dress uniform, my old friend, Dave, remarked that his oldest daughter, Alexis, had also been accepted at the Naval Academy, but after visiting Annapolis she had decided that it was not something she really wanted to do. So she accepted the very prestigious Morehead Scholarship that had been offered to her by the University of North Carolina and was in her freshman year at Chapel Hill.

Alexis is a beautiful young lady, and I remarked to Dave that she would make a wonderful date for one of Bill's friends as they anticipated the traditional Naval Academy Ring Dance scheduled for the following spring. Alexis, however, had a boyfriend she had steadily dated since her freshman year in high school, her father told me, and they were both attending the University of North Carolina that year.

Both of us knew, of course, that the reality of Alexis being in Annapolis, Maryland, for the Ring Dance was extremely remote, and the thought itself was merely a comment, made in passing, meant to reflect how attractive she was and how proud of her and her accomplishments Dave should be.

Several months passed and homecoming weekend became nothing more than a fond memory. On Easter Sunday, in the spring of 2005, I left church with a few friends from the congregation for a golfing trip to Ocean City, Maryland. It had become an annual ritual, and the house we have there in Ocean Pines became our golfing headquarters for those special days.

On Easter Monday evening the phone at the house rang, and much to my surprise it was Dave. He had called our home in Linthicum, and Nancy had given him the number in Ocean Pines. He wanted to tell me that a friend of theirs from their hometown in North Carolina had a son who was graduating from the Naval Academy and was getting married the next day at the Academy Chapel. Dave and his family had been invited to attend the graduation ceremony and the wedding, and since they were going to be in the area, Alexis had mentioned to her Dad that she wouldn't mind being someone's blind date for the Ring Dance, since she had heard so much about the tradition surrounding it.

I was surprised by the unexpected call but told Dave I would ask Bill to see if there was anything he could do about getting her a date.

Bill's first reaction was, "Dad, nobody wants a blind date for the Ring Dance!" But, he agreed to ask around. First, though, he thought he should call her just to find out a little about her and to see what she was like. Ironically, he reached her while she was visiting with her boyfriend. They spoke for about forty-five minutes, I later learned, and Bill was apparently impressed.

Subsequently, I believe, he did make some inquiries among his friends about their need for a date. No one was available. Then, as I remember the story, he spoke with Alexis again, and decided that since he did not yet have a date, and she was the daughter of an old friend of mine, he would ask her to go with him.

The day before the Ring Dance, Dave and Alexis arrived in Annapolis. They had come up a day before the rest of the family in order for Alexis to attend the dance. I met them at the Academy. Bill and his friends were already at a party being held by his roommate whose parents lived near Annapolis. So I drove Dave and Alexis to the party and introduced them to Bill.

Alexis made a great impression on everyone, and the weekend was off to a good start. Bill and his five closest friends had planned things perfectly, and the Ring Dance experience was special for all of them.

But what was really special was the obvious chemistry that immediately existed between my son and my friend's daughter. That chemistry was so obvious, in fact, that by the end of those few fleeting days, a member of my congregation and one of our closest friends there came to Nancy and me and told us, "I am going to plan their bridal shower!"

By the end of that summer, Alexis and her boyfriend had ended their relationship. She and Bill spent as much time together as they could, considering Bill's summer cruise responsibilities and Alexis' fulfillment of the requirements placed upon her by her Morehead Scholarship. In the fall they returned to their respective schools, Bill for the beginning of his last year at the Academy and Alexis for her sophomore year in Chapel Hill.

They continued to see each other, as much as possible, and their relationship grew stronger and stronger. Alexis and her family attended Bill's graduation in 2006, and Alexis, together with Nancy, placed the shoulder boards on his uniform, which represented his commissioning as an Ensign in the United States Navy. After a summer spent on the staff at the Academy, he reported to Surface Warfare School in Newport, Rhode Island. Alexis visited with him there and stayed with my sister and her husband. And it was there on New Year's Eve while taking a chilly stroll on Newport's famous "Cliff Walk" that Bill proposed. They were married in July of 1998, with Dave and me playing significant roles once again. The wedding was held at the Naval Academy Chapel. Dave walked Alexis down the aisle, and I officiated at the ceremony.

A few years later, following Alexis' graduation from law school and Bill's separation from active duty, they eventually settled back in Annapolis where they both have productive, interesting, and busy careers, and where they are raising their two wonderful sons. Both Dave and I acknowledge that God did indeed work through us in a wonderfully special way to bring together two people who were meant for each other and who to this day and forevermore are devoted to one another. We were instruments of God's will for our children and are extremely happy that God gave us that role to play.

In a somewhat less dramatic but just as meaningful way, God also used me to bring my younger son and his wife together. Both Brad and Melissa (Missy) had grown up as members of St. John Lutheran Church in Linthicum, Maryland, with me as their pastor. I confirmed them both, and Missy's mother was one of my long-term Sunday school teachers. Although they were both in church every Sunday, they really never got to know each other. Brad attended a private school away from the Linthicum area, so they didn't move in the same circles throughout their teen years.

Following Brad's graduation from the Naval Academy and his subsequent development as a Naval aviator, he was eventually stationed at the Oceana Naval Air Station near Virginia Beach, Virginia. Occasionally, he would be able to make it home for a weekend, however, and on one of those weekends he was sitting with Nancy during the contemporary worship service on a Sunday morning. A few rows in front of Brad sat an attractive young lady who caught his eye. Following worship he asked me who "the blond was" and I told him it was Missy Jordan.

Some time later Brad was home again for a brief visit. I had a wedding rehearsal on one of the evenings he was there, and since I had something rather awkward that I needed to move from my car to my office, I asked him if he would mind coming to the church when the rehearsal was over to help me. He arrived before the rehearsal had ended to, as he put it, "check out the bridesmaids." One of those bridesmaids happened to be Missy.

They spoke for a few minutes, and Brad was obviously impressed, as was Missy. So the next day he asked if I could get her phone number, which I did.

On Sunday afternoon, the day after the wedding, Brad, Bill and I went out to play golf. We had dinner reservations for that evening for the whole family at a well-known restaurant in Baltimore. As we were playing our round of golf, Brad asked if I would mind having someone else join us, and I said that would be fine. So he called Missy and invited her to dinner, and then called his mother and asked her to make the reservation for one more.

Missy was obviously a good sport. It had to be a bit intimidating for her to go out with him for the first time with his whole family present, especially when his father was also her pastor. But the evening went well, we all enjoyed Missy's company, and after dinner Missy and Brad went out on their own for a while. Something special had begun to develop.

The next night he asked if he could use my tickets to take Missy to the Monday Night Football game the Ravens were playing in Baltimore, and a few weeks later, Missy joined Brad in Virginia for the "Hornet Ball," a formal dance for Naval aviators flying the F-18 Hornet. Her mother told Nancy and me on the Sunday after the dance how excited Missy was about the experience and what a beautiful and special event it had been.

Shortly thereafter, Brad deployed for over six months. They had spent very little time together prior to his departure, but it was apparently enough. Prior to his leaving, he asked his mother to have a dozen roses sent to the school where Missy taught. While he was away, they communicated through email, and, whenever possible, a phone call from overseas. Missy sent him packages, kept a scrapbook for him, and spent some time with Nancy and me as well.

As the day for his return approached, we made plans to be in Virginia when his squadron flew in from the carrier. Friends from church wanted to attend as well, as did Nancy's brother and sister-in-law, and of course Bill, Alexis, and their newborn son, Aiden, whom Brad had not yet met. Missy was also with us, and we all felt very certain that she always would be from that time on.

It was a wonderful homecoming. It was easy to tell that something special was happening for Brad and Missy, and indeed it was. They became engaged a short time later and in July of 2006, they were married. Once again I officiated, as I had for Bill and Alexis. Once again the service was held at the Naval Academy Chapel. And once again I believe that God worked through me to bring together two people he had made for one another. The wonder of God's actions in our lives will always amaze and thrill me.

As my active ministry drew to a close and retirement loomed before me, I found myself reflecting on my thirty-six years in the parish and the concurrent twenty-six I had spent as a reserve Navy chaplain. Those reflective moments served to affirm for me that

God had indeed been guiding my life and providing me, not only with wonderful opportunities for ministry, but also with personal moments and experiences which fulfilled various dreams and visions I had had for my life, even as I fulfilled God's vision for me. I know, without a doubt, that God worked in me and through me, and by so doing, made my life rich and meaningful and a life which I hope was a blessing in some way to others as well.

Indeed, God's grace is amazing, and I am thankful to have known that grace in so many special ways.

An Incredible Journey

As I conclude my reflections on my life and ministry and consider the journey that continues in a new way for me now as a retiree, I am convinced that the course that has been mine to follow is a course God charted for me. It is not a course I have in any way been pre-ordained to follow but a course that God obviously had in mind for me and one, that in sometimes subtle and in other times overt ways, He guided me to take.

Still, since God never forces us to do things His way but continues to allow us the benefit of free choice, I always retained the right to decide the course I would ultimately take in life. Fortunately, in retrospect, the choices I made, though often in conflict with what I might have believed I wanted to do with my life, were always the choices that were best for my life, and I am grateful to God for the guidance He offered.

God, you see, just got to me! He reached out to me through a little jeweled cross embedded in the bark of a tree. He inspired me through a recurring dream to think outside the box I had built around myself and led me to consider the ministry as a vocation. He developed me in ways that enabled me to fulfill that destiny by providing me, in sometimes mysteriously amazing ways, with opportunities to grow as a pastor, build the confidence I needed and lacked to be successful in what He was calling me to do, and continue my education in ways that would enhance my professionalism and my ability to care for those He entrusted to me. He spoke to me with his "still small voice" through the words of mentors and friends, as well as through my own spiritual conscience, and by so doing kept me on course, even in those times when I was tempted to stray from that course. He revealed Himself to me as I sat with those whose last moments on this earth were met with confidence and hope rather than with fear and despair. He showed His unwavering determination to me to fulfill His promise always to be with us as I felt His presence in so many incredible ways during my days at the Pentagon following the horrific events of 9/11. He helped me when illness and death came into my life to threaten those I love by inspiring those who knew me as "pastor" to become a "pastor" to me. He provided me with the one who makes my life complete, my beautiful wife Nancy, and in a uniquely wonderful way. He blessed me with two amazingly gifted and talented sons, who in turn brought two special young ladies into our lives as the daughters we never had, and four beautiful and happy grandchildren.

Consequently, based on my life experiences, if someone would ask me today, "Where is God and why doesn't He speak to us?" I know, without a doubt, what I would tell them. I would say, "Open your eyes! Open your ears! Open your heart! For God is right here with you and always will be. And He is here because He loves you and wants what is best for you. He is here because He has a plan for your life and has charted a course for you to follow if you would just trust Him to show you the way!"

Like everyone else who draws human breath on this earth, I make mistakes. All of my decisions are not always for the best, and

I have known my share of failures as a result. Even King David, the greatest of all the kings of Israel, made mistakes, and his biggest mistake was realized the first time he failed to seek God's counsel and allow God to guide Him. We can and should learn from that truth. For when we allow God to guide our lives, we cannot fail. When we allow God to chart our course, we cannot stray from that which is right and good for us. When we allow God to speak to us, be present with us, and become a part of us, our path through life will be one filled with hope, peace, and joy.

Whatever I might have accomplished in life is not the result of anything I alone was able to achieve. It is purely the result of God taking control of my life and enabling me to do with it what He knew to be right for me, and consequently, beneficial to others. For that I am grateful and reflect now on a life that is full and meaningful and rich.

Your life can be like that too, if you just, "Let God chart your course!"

Notes:

All Biblical quotes are from the *Lutheran Study Bible* (New Revised Standard Version)